The Competitive Advantage - Affecting Leadership for a

Continuous Improvement Culture

By Dr. Charles DesJardins, Ph.D.

www.drcharlesdesjardins@gmail.com

DEDICATION

I owe a debt of gratitude to my wife and children for all the time I took away from them as I worked on learning about Self-Actualization, Neuro-Semantics, and Meta-Coaching. They helped me take responsibility for my own life, and helped me to see that I can change the world by changing myself.

I dedicate this book to two groups of people - to all those giants who have come before me. Without their work and lives that were such an inspiration to me, this book could not have been written. I owe a debt of gratitude to Dr. Michael Hall of the International Society of Neuro-Semantics for his support with my doctoral dissertation and for all the time he took for all the conversations and e-mails that helped bring Neuro-Semantics and Meta-Coaching from my mind to my muscle.

About the Author:

Dr. Charles DesJardins is a Ph.D. in Training and Performance Improvement. He is Certified in Black Belt Six Sigma, Design for Six Sigma, Lean Manufacturing, Associate Meta-Coach, and Self-Actualization (Unleashed).

He has trained hundreds of engineers in Six Sigma and Design for Six Sigma. He teaches business management at several universities at the graduate and undergraduate level. He has started and ran several of his own businesses, retail and consulting.

He is available as a Kaizen Meta-Coach to coach your management team through the Kaizen Meta-Coach Facilitation Process as outlined in this book.

Life is about competing forces on limited resources – use them wisely!

Contents

Introduction

The competitive advantage: Affecting leadership for a continuous improvement culture is a book about a model for affecting leadership in such a way that they engender a cultural revolution that supports the process of continuous improvement. The model is a prescription of the creation of a gestalt that offers one more competitive advantage, that is, the development of a continuous improvement culture.

This book is about the facilitation of a natural continuous improvement systemic process which garners relevant information from many sources and from many cultures (management theory, leadership theory, performance theory, psychological theory, etc.). This book is about a system that uses and facilitates the latest (which also includes seminal thinkers) theories and applications and integrates them into a workable model that will give your organization a competitive advantage of continuous improvement through the means of affecting the leadership of the organization. This book is both theory and practice. It lays out a path and a model for developing a culture, through leadership, of continuous improvement. In this book you will find old and new ideas. It is not the ideas that will make this happen; many have these ideas but still cannot translate them into a workable continuous improvement culture, it is the synthesis of these ideas into a model of a new gestalt that will have a competitive advantage of effective leadership.

This book will focus on several key themes and from those themes a workable, applicable, and relevant model will emerge. The key themes in this book are culture, leadership, cognition to behavior, continuous improvement, self-actualization, and coaching using the Meta-Coaching Model.

What do culture, leadership, cognition to behavior, continuous improvement, self-actualization, and the Meta-Coach facilitation process have to do with each other? If they have something to do with each other, how are they expressed in a model that would give an organization a competitive advantage?

This book defines culture as shared norms, values, and beliefs of a group of people. Societies, businesses, families, clans, etc. have culture. If culture is the shared norms, values, and beliefs of a group of people, then those norms, values, and beliefs will drive the behavior of that group. This book is particularly looking at business organizations and the culture of those organizations. If an organization, through its leadership, needs to create a specific set of behaviors to meet some specific demands that meet their customer's needs, then they need to affect the norms, the values, and the beliefs of those people who need to behave in a specific manner that meet those customer needs and ultimately, give the organization a competitive advantage.

Leadership, at least in this book, states that leadership is not management. Managers can be leaders, or cannot be leaders. Leaders can be managers, or leaders can be 'not managers'. Leadership is that ability to influence people. To lead people and influence people who would not otherwise have been influenced. Organizations are guided and driven by leaders, be they leaders in positional power, or leaders in personal power. Leadership is not always a positional thing, that is, an official title. Leaders can come from the employee, an employee who has personal power and who influences people to behave in specific ways within the organization. This book and this new model are about leaders who have both positional and personal power. The book is for those in a business position to lead and guide and influence organizational behavior toward the organizations goals – in this case, toward continuous improvement.

Cognition to behavior is another way of saying, transfer of training. Continuous improvement is both philosophical as well as technical. Tools and methods such as Six Sigma, Design for Six Sigma, Lean Manufacturing, etc. are all methods that need to be taught to those who will use them. Training someone in these continuous improvement tools or methods does not necessarily change his or her behavior. Training only delivers knowledge, but does not necessarily change behavior. The new model in this book includes the assurance of an episodic cognition that takes place through the training and then a transfer of that training into measurable and repeatable behavior.

Continuous Improvement, often known as Kaizen, is a step-by-step method for being in the continual flow of improvement. Kaizen is the attitude that the current process, product, or structure is never good enough; improvement can always take place. At the start then, Continuous Improvement is not just a set of steps, or a set of methods, or a set of tools; it is rather a philosophy.

Self-Actualization is a process of being. Self-Actualization takes place at the individual level, the business level, the social level, and the political level. Self-Actualization is the process of reaching full growth. For the individual, Self-Actualization takes place as that person's lower deficiency needs are met and the individual moves toward the growth needs. As it relates to business and to this model in specific, self-actualization occurs when a person performs at his or her best; he or she adds the highest meanings to his or her performance and adds performance to his or her highest meanings, he or she become peak performers.

The Meta-Coach is a trained person in the structure and process of Continuous Improvement engendered by the Self-Actualization of the person and the organization. The Meta-Coach has seven models that he or she uses to facilitate Continuous Improvement, through the Self-Actualization of the individual and the organization.

I will now ask again, what do culture, leadership, cognition to behavior, continuous improvement, self-actualization, and the Meta-Coach facilitation process have to do with each other?

Everything.

Leadership can come under the control of culture and also establish culture. Culture, expressed through leadership affects transfer of training. The use of continuous improvement in a continuously sustained way for a competitive advantage must be the culture of the organization. The continuous improvement process is done by people; self-actualization psychology, practiced and facilitated by the Meta-Coach process, brings together the highest performance of the employee and leader, who now are a planned part of the culture. The results of this model of transformation is that you have a gestalt of continuous improvement of culture, continuous improvement of leadership, continuous improvement of cognition to behavior all bringing forth a continuous improvement of the organization, of which, you have the competitive advantage.

The relationship between culture, leaders, self-actualization, motivation, training, etc and the need for organizations who want to exceed and excel in their competitive advantage is understanding the need for change in all three core areas of the business, and those core areas are (1) the work to be done, (2) the worker who does that work, and (3) the workplace itself. That is why the Meta-Coach Kaizen facilitation process includes senior management, middle managers, and the floor worker, for it takes Kaizen change in all of them to ensure change in the work, worker, and workplace.

Superior organizational performance is the result of systemic continuous improvement of three core areas of the organization. To experience this superior performance the organization must continually improve the work to be done, the worker who is to do the work, and the workplace in which the work will be done. This continuous improvement is predicated on leadership's ability to have well formed mental models that drive this systemic change.

Mental models exist within a framework of behavior and are pushed and pulled by the level of growth or motivation of those leaders. Does the mental model that drives behavior exist within the deficiency needs of the leader, or do these mental models exist and facilitate the growth needs of the leaders?

The self-actualization literature predicates that the process of self-actualization is a growth process and this process is facilitated by, and facilitates specific mental models and specific overt behaviors. Research has shown that Meta-Coach training engenders this facilitation process of self-actualization and this self-actualization has a positive effect on business leader's organization performance.

Chapter One

Continuous Improvement

What type of Continuous Improvement are we discussing here?
Continuous Improvement can be called by different names and with different ways in which to continually improve. Continuous improvement has been called Lean Manufacturing, and some of the tools of Lean Manufacturing are 5s, value stream mapping, single minute of exchange dies (SMED), total productive maintenance (TPM), Six Sigma, and Design for Six Sigma.

Other tools and methods that are used to continually improve an organization; some of those other subsets or tools are Hoshin Planning, standardized work, Jidoka, mistake proofing, and just in time.

The Continuous Improvement Philosophy is often called Kaizen. Kaizen is a Japanese word that means "improvement." When Kaizen is applied at the business organizational level, it reflects a continual improvement from the manufacturing floor all the way to the CEO's office. The word Kaizen and the *'meaning'* that lies

13

behind the word is more than simply to continually improve. The word as used in this book as well as the connotation of the word in Japanese reflects the inclusion of human resources in the continually improved process. "Kaizen epitomizes the mobilisation (sic) of the work force, providing the main channel for employees to contribute to their company's development."[1] Similarities exist between the Japanese word 'Kaizen' and the philosophical implication of that word have in common with the past work of Mayo, Maslow, McGregor, Argyris and Herzberg.[2]

Behind the word and philosophy of Kaizen, is an integrative activity, proffered as a system of activities that flow from the intrinsic psychological outlook of the employees. Kaizen takes place within the sphere of employee satisfaction, employee motivation; motivation and satisfaction that has been and can be modeled from the works of Mayo, Maslow, McGregor, Argyris and Herzberg. Kaizen, then, is an imbedded psychology and philosophy in the minds of management and employees. It has been stated that, "the concept is so deeply ingrained in the minds of both managers and

---

[1] Brunet, A. P., & New, S. (2003). Kaizen in Japan: an empirical study. *International Journal of Operations & Production Management.* 23(11/12).
[2] Brunet, A. P., & New, S. (2003). Kaizen in Japan: an empirical study. *International Journal of Operations & Production Management.* 23(11/12).

workers that they often do not even realize that they are thinking *kaizen.*" [3]

What is the purpose of Kaizen?

Obviously with all the tools, methods, and activities that facilitate Kaizen, one could ask, why even use Kaizen? The general reasons for using Kaizen are:

1. Giving the customer exactly what he or she wants – In most manufacturing situations there are customer specifications that need to be met. The product must meet some type of requirement and an organization must ensure that they meet or exceed that specification.

2. Reliable – Serves the length of purpose for which it was created. Customers expect that a product will last for a certain amount of time. The product must meet or exceed the length and durability that the customer expects.

3. In the time that the customer wants it- Customers have specific times that they want their product. Many

---

[3] Imai, M. (1986). *kaizen: The key to Japanese competitive success.* New York: McGraw Hill.

companies have set up just in time processes in which they ship the product just in time for the end customer. Just in time requires a lean manufacturing process as well as a strategic logistics process.

4. Free of defects – The product and every part of the component of that product must be free of defects. Each piece of an assembly has variation in the process that causes variation in the product. When an organization builds an assembly that has multiple parts, some manufactured by them and some purchased from suppliers, they have the possibility of manufacturing, building, and shipping a product with a defect.

5. At the lowest cost – Costs of a product are in the materials, the engineering, the design, the manufacturing, the packaging, the shipping, etc. All these costs must be managed through the Kaizen process.

6. With the least inventory – Inventory is money. When product sits in inventory, it cuts into the cash flow of an organization. Kaizen includes manufacturing parts in a one piece flow system.

7. With the best manufacturing processes – Manufacturing includes making parts, assembling parts, moving parts, checking parts, packaging parts, etc. Each step in that process affects the cost, the quality, the reliability, the availability, etc. and needs to be continually improved.

8. With the least manpower – Production and assembly lines are usually manned by people. Manufacturing plants are manned by people. Shipping and receiving are manned by people. A lean office or a lean manufacturing facility requires less manpower and thus less costs.

9. With the best (quality and low cost) materials – Parts are made from materials. Materials can be produced at the manufacturing plant level or purchased from a materials supplier. Part of the Kaizen process is to look for ways to use the best materials at the lowest cost. Products may be redesigned to use less material. Plastics may have different materials for different applications.

10. With the best engineering practices – there are many ways to engineer a part. Seventy five percent of the cost of a product is designed into the part. An engineering process that engineers a part for design, for assembly, for reliability,

for durability, for variation control, etc. is a Kaizen engineering process.

11. With little waste in the process- Manufactured parts may have extra material at the gates, may have production lines not set up such that they are efficient, they may have parts for an assembly located far from the line, they may waste time changing over dies, etc. This process needs to be continually reviewed for improvements.

Kaizen is about always looking, finding, and implementing ways to add more value to the customer for fewer costs.

Kaizen is not just for manufacturing organizations

Kaizen is no longer just a philosophy of manufacturing firms. Retail stores, hospitals, service industries, legal firms, etc. are all realizing and finding ways to continually improve on their human capital and their processes. Organizations other than manufacturing organizations are realizing that just hiring the right people is not enough to have the right processes for those right people. Many different service industries are sending people to Japan or other places where the Toyota Production System (TPS) is being used. These organizations are then taking these principles of TPS and the other Kaizen methods and tools and integrating them into their organizations.

Lean Enterprise, Lean Office, and Six Sigma Transactional are all processes or tools that organizations are using to add Kaizen to their service or non-manufacturing organizations.

How Kaizen is implemented

Manufacturing and non-manufacturing organizations face similar challenges when they implement Kaizen. Most organizations start off the same, but go off in divergent ways as they progress on that track of Kaizen. Some organizations bring in consultants and then bring in trainers or send their executive team out for training. Many consulting and training organizations certify people in all the tools and processes of Kaizen. Once organizations have their key personnel trained, they then tend to develop their own training systems and do their own internal training. Many organizations develop training superior to the outside training that they received because the training becomes developed around the specific needs of the organization.

Then what happens?

Many organizations are challenged concerning maintaining a culture of Kaizen. It is one thing to train your executives, middle management, and engineers or others, and quite another thing to ensure that all this training gets transferred back to the workplace.

It is critical, mission critical, for any and all Kaizen initiatives to become part of the organization's mission and vision and specifically, its culture. Jeffrey Pfeffer, of Standford University, when discussing the success of Southwest Airline stated that "it's the philosophy and not the techniques" that gave Southwest its competitive advantage. And it is still so, it is the philosophy, and not necessarily the technique. This is not to say that the techniques are not important, but that the techniques without the philosophy will not get you the results that you need to maintain that competitive advantage.

It is therefore of much importance to have a starting place in the development of this facilitation process. Affecting leadership takes the affecter as well as those affected to act in specific ways; to make a movement in one direction or the other. A person can stand still, go backwards, or move forward (they can go up or down or sideways, but we will limit this discussion) and this movement can be solidified or nominalized by work motivation. Given that an organization needs to have all those involved in the Kaizen process to make a movement in that direction, it is important to understand theories of motivation.

Chapter Two

The Motivation of the People behind Continuous Improvement

In the last chapter it was pointed out that there are close similarities between the word 'Kaizen' and the philosophical implications of that word with the works of Mayo, Maslow, McGregor, Argyris and Herzberg. The works of Mayo, Maslow, McGregor, Argyris and Herzberg, etc. are works that focus on individual and employee behavior. What this alludes to is that a true Kaizen initiative must include the natural desire and proclivity of the employee toward change.

Change takes place both in the employee and through the employee as the employee has motive to move out in a specific direction. Mayo, Maslow, McGregor, Argyris and Herzberg, etc., each had different theories on what and how employees are motivated. It is important to understand how people are motivated and then it is important to further understand how this motivation really works.

There are basically three different approaches for explaining motivated behavior[4]. There are needs based approaches, there are cognitive based approaches, and there are non-cognitive based approaches.

Motivation is the moving out to do something and in any change initiative it is critical to understand that motivation is a potential performance improvement initiative.[5] Part of a successful transfer of Continuous Improvement training plan includes affecting the motivation behind attitudes and abilities of the trainee.[6] As with most processes, the Kaizen process uses highly technical training courses that when transferred back to the work place are a mixture of both near and far transfer.

Needs Based Motivation Theories

---

[4] Desimone, R. L., Werner, J. M., & Harris, D.M. (2002). *Human resource development*. (3rd ed.) New York: Harcourt College Publishers.

[5] Gilbert, T. F. (1996). *Human competence: Engineering worth performance*. Washington, DC: Human Resource Development Press and International Society for Performance Improvement.
Harless, J. H. (1979). *Front-end analysis of soft skills training*. Newnan, GA: Harless Performance Guild.

[6] Baldwin, T. T., & Ford, J. K. (1988). Transfer of training. A review and directions for future research. *Personnel psychology, 41*, 63-105.

Needs based motivational theories postulate that people have basic needs and that they act or behave in such a way so as to meet those needs. The premise of one hierarchical needs based theory presumes that once a particular lower need is met, then the individual's behavior is driven to meet the next higher level need.

Another hierarchical needs based theory allows for a mixture of needs fulfillment. A third needs based theory postulates that some needs act as hygiene factors and another set act as motivators. The first of the two hierarchal needs based theories is Maslow's Hierarchy of Needs theory.[7] The second widely discussed hierarchal needs based theory is Alderfer's existence, relatedness, and growth (ERG) theory.[8] The third needs based motivational theory that is widely discussed is Herzberg's two factor theory.[9]

Maslow's Hierarchy of Needs Theory

Maslow proposed a theory of motivation that was based on behavioral changes driven by the current needs of the individual

---

[7] Maslow, A. H. (1968). *Toward a psychology of being.* (2nd Ed.) New York: Van Nostrand Reinhold.

[8] Alderfer, C. P. (1972). *Existence, relatedness, and growth.* New York: Free Press.

[9] Herzberg, F. H. (1966). *Work and the nature of man.* Cleveland: World Publishing Company.

and the need to continually have and fulfill needs.[10] Maslow categorized these needs into two different groupings: deficiency needs and growth needs. Maslow proposed that until the lower level needs are fulfilled, the individual will not seek to fulfill the higher needs. The deficiency needs are such that if not satisfied the other higher needs will not emerge. Maslow further delineated the needs based groupings into five levels: physiological, safety and security, love, status and esteem, and self actualization.

Physiology is having the basic needs of food and water met. Maslow proposed that until a person has enough food to eat or water to drink that person will not be motivated by the other needs. If the stomach is empty or the mouth is parched, the idea of security or love is not the idea that would drive behavior, the desire for food and water would drive behavior.

---

[10] Maslow, A. H. (1943). *A theory of human motivation.* from
    http://psychclassics.yorku.ca/Maslow/motivation.htm

The next need on Maslow's hierarchy is safety and security. Once a person has the basic need of food and water taken care of, that person will next seek safety and security. In context, once a person has a job that can pay the bills and feed the family, the next need that is satiated by desire is the need for safety and security; a job in which a person feels safe and will experience career longevity. Company pensions and seniority may meet those needs. Once the person has the needs of safety and security met, those needs no longer drive behavior but the next are status and esteem.

Again in context, once a person feels safe and secure that person will seek out for love, social interaction, or belongingness. There will be a need for social bonding. As it pertains to work, this entails relationships with others at work. Again in context, once a person feels loved, the next motivational need is to have status and with that, self esteem. If any of the other needs that came prior to status and esteem return (physiology, safety and security) the individual will again revert back to meeting those needs before continuing on with status and esteem. After the status and esteem are met, a person will move to levels of self-actualization. Not all people will go through all of these phases; some may never have the prior phase met so they do not move on to the next level.[11]

Alderfer's ERG Theory

Another needs based theory that is similar to Maslow's needs based theory is Alderfer's ERG theory. Even though the theories are similar and both are based on needs, Alderfer's ERG is not set up where one level must be fulfilled before the next, but the core needs may exist simultaneously. It is this difference where Alderfer's ERG theory complements Maslow's theory into three core needs.[12] Alderfer's revised version of Maslow's Hierarchy of Needs centers around the core needs of: Existence, Relatedness, and Growth.[13] Alderfer's existence can correspond to Maslow's physiology and safety needs; relatedness can correspond to Maslow's social needs and Alderfer's growth needs can correspond to Maslow's esteem and self-actualization needs. The biggest difference between Alderfer's ERG theory and Maslow's Hierarchy

[11] Huitt, W. (2004). Maslow's hierarchy of needs. *Educational Psychology Interactive*. Valdosta, GA: Valdosta State University. Retrieved from http://chiron.valdosta.edu/whuitt/col/regsys/maslow.html

[12] Hersey, P., Blanchard, K. H., & Johnson, D. E. (2001). *Management of organizational behavior: Leading human resources*. (8th ed.). Upper Saddle River, NJ: Prentice Hall.

[13] Alderfer, C. P. (1969). An empirical test of a new theory of human needs. *Organizational Behavior and Human Performance, 4*, 142-175.

of Needs theory is that Maslow's theory proposes that only one of the needs will be predominate at one time (although Maslow did recognize that needs can overlap) while with Alderfer's ERG theory, any of the needs can be active at the same time.

Herzberg's Two Factor Theory

Another needs based motivational theory was proposed by Herzberg. Herzberg theorized that there are two sets of needs: survival, and growth.[14] Both Maslow and Alderfer postulated needs that were based on survival and on growth. Where the major difference exists between Herzberg's theory and the other two was that Herzberg theorized that the survival needs were hygienic while the growth needs were motivational; the hygiene needs were more animalistic where the growth needs were more human. The theory basically states that if a worker is to have satisfaction than offer them the survival needs. These are not motivators; they are hygiene factors that keep employees from being dissatisfied. The motivators are in the area of growth. Without growth, you have no

---

[14] Herzberg, F. H. (1966). *Work and the nature of man*. Cleveland: World Publishing Company.

motivation. You need growth for satisfaction and survival to keep from dissatisfaction.

Cognitive Based Motivation

Cognitive based motivational theories, being different than needs based theories, espouse a thinking person; a person with on-going cognitive processes and one who uses these processes with meta-awareness that directs the behavior of that individual. It is in the domain of cognitive science and the research findings from that science that defines the cognitive process of understanding. "Cognitive science attempts to understand the way our thoughts and our perceptions of information influence our understanding." [15] Cognitive science delves into the mysteries of the cognitive processes as they relate to things such as an individual's "eagerness, readiness, and enthusiasm." [16] It is "argued that

---

[15] Clark, R. E. (1999). The cognitive sciences and human performance technology. In H. D. Stolovitch & E. J. Keeps (Eds.), *Handbook of human performance technology: Improvin individual and organizational performance worldwide* (pp. 82-95). San Francisco, CA: Pfeiffer.

[16] Rossett, A. (1999). Analysis for human performance technology. In H. D. Stolovitch & E. J. Keeps (Eds.). *Handbook of human performance technology: Improving individual and ,organizational performance worldwide* (pp. 139-162). San Francisco, CA: Pfeiffer. P. 158

motivation is based on a person's thoughts and beliefs (or cognitions)." [17]

Expectancy Theory

Motivation is a process; it is a conscious choice.[18] Here you have the start of the expectancy theory that was suggested by Vroom. At the heart of expectancy is the idea that an individual will make an effort to accomplish something if that individual believes that it can be accomplished. There is an expectation by the individual that effort put forth will result in some positive experience. Expectancy theory has three elements of belief: valence, instrumentality, and expectancy. In cognitive based theories of motivation there are content and process theories of motivation; expectancy is a process theory of motivation in which expectancy theory is based on extrinsic motivators. It is in external rewards and expectation of things from the outside that drive expectancy motivation.

The expectancy element of the expectancy theory basically states that a person will only be motivated to do that which the person

---

[17] Desimone, R. L., Werner, J. M., & Harris, D.M. (2002). *Human resource development*. (3rd ed.) New York: Harcourt College Publishers.

[18] Vroom, V. H. (1964). *Work and motivation*. New York: Wiley

feels competent to do. If the person believes that by using effort a performance goal will be achieved, that person will perform that effort. If that person does not believe that an effort will lead to performance, that person will not perform that effort.

The instrumentality element of expectancy theory is a belief that if an individual performs an effort that the effort will result in an outcome. If an individual believes that it is possible for them to paint a fence in four hours (expectancy) and that the effort of painting will accomplish the goal; that is instrumentality.

The valence element of the expectancy theory is the belief that if an individual performs an effort, the results of that effort are something that the individual values; that is, it is worth the effort. Expending four hours effort to paint a friends fence may not have valence and thus the effort may not be expended. If, expending four hours to paint one's own fence and thus increase the value or esthetics of the fence and that is valuable to the individual, then the individual will expend that effort.

Goal Setting Theory

"Behavior is basically goal oriented." [19] A goal is what a person sets out to accomplish; moving toward something.[20] Goal setting theory states that having goals for performance will enhance and have a motivational affect on the performance of those goals. Goal setting theory is a well supported theory through research and in the literature. Research with goal setting theory has confirmed three critical characteristics of successful goal setting strategies. If the workforce has a commitment to achieving goals then it is better to have difficult goals than easy ones and it is better to have specific goals than to have non-specific goals.[21] And it is critical that feedback is giving for any performance improvement that was motivated by a goal.

Goal setting theory includes the concept that in a work place setting it is a realistic goal that is accomplishable that will give the

---

[19] Hersey, P., Blanchard, K. H., & Johnson, D. E. (2001). *Management of organizational behavior: Leading human resources*. (8th ed.). Upper Saddle River, NJ: Prentice Hall.

[20] Locke, E.A. (1968). Toward a theory of task motivation and incentives. *Organisational Behaviour and Human Performance, 3,* 157-189.

[21] Locke, E.A. & Latham, G.P. (1990). *A theory of goal-setting and task performance*. Englewood Cliffs: Prentice-Hall.

employee a sense of accomplishment. [22] Goals need to be stated clearly, they must be challenging, they must be accomplishable, and the performance toward the goal must include a feedback process.

Equity Theory

Equity theory is also known as Adams Equity Theory, named after a behavioral psychologist who developed the equity theory in 1963.

Equity theory states that people want to be treated fairly. If people believe that they are treated fairly or equitably, they will be motivated by such treatment. There are three main perceptual components or assumptions of equity theory: The person has a perceived personal value and that the person believes that value is recognized by others and thus that person in turn returns value back.

The second assumption is that this perception is usually developed by how the person feels others are treated and that is used as a

---

[22] Gorman, P. (2003). *Motivation and emotion.* New York: Routledge.

datum point. The person compares how much activity is put forth and what is received for that activity compared to what others do and receive for that doing. Equity theory would predict that if a person perceives being treated well or better than others, that may motivate that person. If that person perceives being treated worse than others, the person will not be motivated. The third assumption is that if the person believes they are being treated unfairly, that person will try to find ways to reduce the inequity.

According to equity theory, if people believe that the treatment received is fair, that person will continue to maximize performance. If that person believes that treatment is unfair that person will find a way to reduce this feeling. The person may distort reality; influence others to reduce performance to bring equity back, change behavior either for better or for worse, change who they compare themselves to, and or just leaving the situation. If there are employees who do not feel the reception of equitability and yet do not leave the company, research has shown that there is an opportunity for misbehavior and even theft from the company.[23]

---

[23] Vardi, Y., & Weitz, E. (2004). *Misbehavior in organizations: Theory, research, and management.* Mahwah, NJ: Lawrence Erlbaum Associates.

Comparison and Contrasts Between Needs Based with Cognitive Based Motivation Theories

Comparisons

The most likely comparison between needs based and cognitive based motivational theories are that the theories are about behavior and what drives that behavior. Needs based and cognitive based theories of motivation have physiological and psychological underpinning. A needs based theory of motivation has postulated that people have needs that they want met; these needs can be physical or psychological. If people have needs, to fulfill those needs, one needs to act, and thus to behave in a specific manner to satisfy that need. This holds for cognitive based theories of motivation as well. If a person is evaluating fairness or equitability, that equitability may include pay for work and pay (money) may also be a need that the individual has at that time.

When comparing the need for social status or self esteem gained by social interaction, the needs based motivational theories can be used to describe this. Maslow and Alderfer both explained that at some time people have needs for relatedness or social status. Both expectancy theory and goal setting theory could also be theories that explain the need or desire for relatedness or social status. Life coaching has become a popular way for people to change and grow and coaches work with people to set goals. Some of these goals are challenges and a goal may be to meet a need. When a goal is set and that goal, according to goal setting theory, meets a need of attaining social status, you have both goal setting and needs based motivation working together.

Even though there is a difference between needs based motivation and cognitive based motivation, both can integrate to explain behavior. Both are about what motivates an individual to change. If it is a need, there will be a drive to fulfill that need. That drive may take the form of valence in expectancy theory and thus between believing in the value of changing behavior and in the value of what is obtained from changing behavior, you have a compounded motivational theory.

Contrasts within Needs Based Theories

Within the needs based theories of motivation there are contrasted differences. Maslow's theory of motivation is hierarchical stating that the higher level needs are not sought after until the lower level needs are met. Alderfer's ERG theory aligns with Maslow's needs, yet Aderfer did not state that the lower needs need to be satisfied before the higher needs. According to Alderfer the needs of existence, relatedness, and growth, can all operate at the same time or at different times. Herzberg even contrasted with both Maslow and Alderfer by believing that some needs are not motivational, the needs simply need to exist so a person is not un-motivated.

Contrasts within Cognitive Based Theories

Within the cognitive based needs theories of motivation there are contrasted differences. Equity theory contrasts with expectancy theory by the fact that according to equity theory, for a person to be motivated, that person must perceive that others treat them fairly; while expectancy relates to the goal and not the perception of fairness in pursuit of that goal.

Expectancy theory has three components and one of the components is expectancy toward the ability to perform a behavior. Equity theory postulates that a person will be motivated to perform that behavior as long as they believe they are being treated fairly, while expectancy theory postulates that the person will only perform that behavior if they believe that they can. Goal setting theory contrasts with both expectancy and equity theory by reason that motivation is driven by a goal, and not a deficiency.

Goals exist because a person is not where they want to be. According to goal setting theory, if a goal that can be obtained is set, the person will behave as to meet that goal and that goal may overcome both the perception of inequity and the perception of expectancy; goal setting can actually spring board from those two other behavioral deficiencies.

Contrast between Theories

Needs based theories of motivation postulate that people are motivated by needs. There is either a bodily function (like hunger pains) type of needs or there can even be cognitive functioning needs (like self-actualization). There is some type of physical or mental need whose outcome is of interest and of which needs to be satisfied.[24] Wherein with cognitive based motivational theories it is not specific needs that are the motivating force but rather beliefs and perceptions about equity, or about expectancy, or even about the need to reach a goal.

Needs based theories propagate the motivation process in a way that behavior is modified when there is an unsatisfied need. This unsatisfied need will cause tension within the individual. That tension creates a drive for fulfillment. Behavior is modified or directed toward that fulfillment. If the behavior is such that it satisfies that fulfillment, then the need is satisfied and the tension is reduced.

There is a greater difference between the different cognitive based families of motivation than there is for the needs based families of motivational theories. The key common theme that contrasts the needs based theories with the three cognitive based theories is that

---

[24] Robbins, S. P. (2004). *Essentials of organizational behavior.* Upper Saddle River, New Jersey: Prentice Hall.

the cognitive based theories all operate from a cognitive-meta-awareness position rather than a needs awareness position.

Cognitive based motivational theories propagate the process of perceptions and beliefs rather than driven by needs. Finally, given that there are commonalities and interaction potential between the different theories of motivation, a model that affects consideration of these main theories is an important part of the Kaizen, Self-Actualization, and Meta-Coach model.

The Axis of Change

Given that there are different theories of motivation and given that they compare in some points and contrast in others, is it possible to have one theory or motivation or one way to use some or all of the types of motivation as a method of change? If some people are motivated to change based on a physical need and if others are motivated to change because they *'think'* about things that are important to them before they make that change. If some people need goals to make change, then what is the leader to do to facilitate the change that would bring about a *'Kaizen'* type of behavior in the individual and in the organization?

40

The Axis of Change

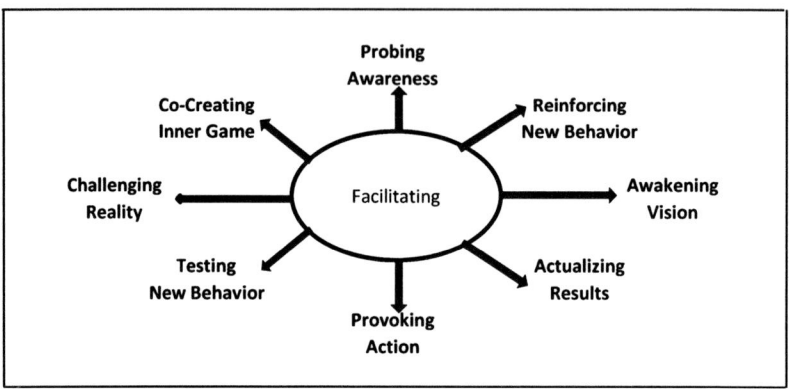

The Axis of Change Model (Hall & Duval, 2004).

The Axis of Change Model is a model of how people naturally change. A person can be in many different states when they decide to make a change. In the context of Kaizen and the necessary change that is required in the development of a Kaizen culture, that is, real Kaizen culture, all levels of the organization must change.

If we follow the outline of this book and reflect back on how individual and corporate motivation takes place, the Axis of Change Model tracks and facilitates the change through the natural change process. The first Axis on the Axis of Change Model is the Axis of Motivation.

Given that it has been highlighted that individuals may be motivated either through a process of needs, cognitive processes, or non-cognitive (goal based), it becomes apparent that whatever is the driving motivation of an individual, that individual will either behave in such a way that they are moving away from something, or moving toward something. It does not matter what process they use or where they fit in the needs or cognitive based process, but are they trying to move away from something, or are they trying to move toward something, or maybe a bit of both.

The Axis of Change Model tracks and facilitates that movement. The Axis of Change Model facilitates that motivation because it apprehends this key component of changes in behavior. Every person within an organization, who is responsible to fulfill the corporate Kaizen mission and thus a Kaizen event, will either move away from something or they will move toward something.

Once an employee or management personnel are trained in any of the Continuous Improvement tools and processes, they are, or may be, challenged to move out with that new information. Will your worker, middle manager, or senior executive implement within their neurology Kaizen because they are moving away from something or because they are moving toward something? The Axis of Change Model tracks and facilitates this process by creating a synergy between all the different motivational theories, between the individual's propulsion system, and the strategic goals of the organization.

No senior executive, no middle manager, and no employee will modify their behavior in such a manner to bring about a desired organizational result without first contemplating and then acting in such a way that they are moving away from something that they can no longer deal with, or moving toward something that they must have. In your Kaizen process, do you create a propulsion system that moves your executive, your middle manager, and your employees away from some specific event or idea toward some specific event or idea?

The organizational results we get are predicated on the behavior of senior, middle, and lower level employees. And behavior is predicated on which type of motivation, needs, cognitive, non-cognitive, drive the individual. Once it is known what type of motivation your executive, middle manager, and employee emote from, then the next step is to heat up the motivation either by challenging your executive, middle manager, or employee if they need to move away from the cost of poor quality, poor processes, poor production capabilities etc.; or to awaken your executive, middle manager, or employees to move toward quality, defect free processes, and efficient production processes.

Motivation is one of the key Axis's of the Axis of Change Model. The Axis of Change Model is a model of how people naturally change. The model is a leverage point for senior executives, middle managers, consultants, and coaches to facilitate the motivational change of the individual. Through the use of this first Axis, your executive, middle manager and employee becomes, through the action of their new belief's, true Kaizen individuals.

The results are a move toward a competitive advantage gained through the lived implementation of Kaizen. Do we dare believe it is possible? What do we need to move away from to believe? What do we need to move toward to believe? What happens if we do not believe? Can we sustain our competitive advantage if we do not move away from poor quality, from inefficient processes? What will happen if we do believe? What will happen to our competitive advantage if we improve our quality and increase our efficiencies? We have moved away, we have moved toward, what now?

The appearance of a motivational strategy and a model to facilitate this process becomes apparent when the employee takes place in some type of training program to get them the skills they need to perform Kaizen. But, if training only gives knowledge and does not necessarily change the behavior of those trained, then what type action is necessary to transfer what the learner has learned into the organization? What role does the leader or senior executive play in this transfer? How do we facilitate that and how do we measure the success of that?

Chapter Three

Transfer of Training

Having looked at a brief description of Kaizen, after looking at various theories of motivation and the Axis of Change model to facilitate the away from/toward aspect of motivation, it is now critical to look at movement of the inner game to the outer game. The inner game is the motivation of your executive, middle manager, and employee and the outer game is the transfer of the Kaizen knowledge, garnered from formal training into the work place.

A critical component of developing a Kaizen culture is multi-tiered. At the first level it is critical that any training that takes place gets transferred back to that work place. The transfer of training requires the close interaction of the trainer, the trainee, and management. A few models of transfer will be reviewed. It is not the intention to recommend that every company follow the transfer models as outlined, but rather that a view toward ensuring transfer takes place.

With less than about 10% of training getting transferred back to the work place[25] it is critical to develop a transfer of training model to ensure transfer and to evaluate the effectiveness of that intervention.[26] Various models and methods of evaluation have been suggested.[27] Phillips ROI model of evaluation has become popular as a standardized method to follow for training evaluation and is now used in hundreds of businesses and in over 40 different countries.[28]

Phillips ROI model is not the only model that exists to measure evaluation; in fact, there are models that desire to go beyond Phillips ROI model.[29] Others go even further and state that learning

[25] Baldwin, T. T., & Ford, J. K. (1988). Transfer of training. A review and directions for future research. *Personnel psychology, 41,* 63-105.

25. Hofman, F. O. (1983). Is management doing the job? *Training and Development Journal, 37*(1), 34-39.

[26] Barksdale, S. & Lund, T. (2001). *Rapid evaluation.* Alexandria, VA: ASTD.

[27] Barksdale, S. & Lund, T. (2001). *Rapid evaluation.* Alexandria, VA: ASTD.

27. Morrison, G. R., Ross, S. M., & Kemp, J. E. (2004). *Designing effective instruction.* (4th ed.).

27. Phillips, J. J. (1997). *Handbook of training evaluation and measurement methods* (3rd ed.). Houston, TX: Gulf Publishing.

27. Phillips, J. L. & Stone, R. D. (2002). *How to measure training results: A practical guide to tracking the six key indicators.* New York: McGraw Hill.

[28] Phillips, J. L. & Stone, R. D. (2002). *How to measure training results: A practical guide to tracking the six key indicators.* New York: McGraw Hill.

28. Stone, R. (2006). Training magazines training solutions conference & expo. *Training, 43*(7)

[29] Pangarker, A., & Kirkwood, T. (2006). Beyond ROI: Alternate measures. *Chief Learning Officer, 5*(11), 36-43.

should be considered as its own business unit, a unit within a unit and that means there should be continual data collection, dashboards, and score cards.[30] There are at least nine different frameworks for evaluation and each frame work has some different criteria than the others, and than that of Phillips.[31]

Part of the Kaizen process includes training individuals in certain methodologies and tools that will ultimately lead to process or product improvements. Like any training, Kaizen training must be transferred back to the work place for it to have any value for the organization. Given that there are models or approaches that are different from the Phillips ROI model, an analysis of Phillips ROI model and a comparison of that model with others are reviewed.

Phillips ROI Model

The Phillips ROI model has its historical foundation in Kirkpatrick's model. As early as 1959 Kirkpatrick was proposing a four step model of evaluation. Kirkpatrick defined a model of evaluation that

---

[30] Davenport, R. (2006, April). In God we trust; all others bring data. *T & D, 60*(4), 45-47.

[31] Desimone, R. L., Werner, J. M., & Harris, D.M. (2002). *Human resource development.* (3rd ed.) New York: Harcourt College Publishers.

consisted of four levels. Kirkpatrick stated that to measure the impact of training one needs to measure the reaction of the training, the learning from the training, behavior of the trainees once back on the job, and the impact that the behavior has on the company. The Phillips ROI model adds a fifth level (measuring the ROI) to the four levels of evaluation that was developed by Kirkpatrick.

The framework that exists for the Phillips ROI model is made up of five different levels; expanding on the Kirkpatrick model. Data should be collected at each of these levels. That data can be hard data or soft data. Hard data can be categorized into four areas: The measure of increased output, the measurement of improved quality, the reduction or improvement of costs, and the savings of time. Soft data can be categorized into six different areas: The measure of change in work habits, a measure of a change in the work climate or environment, a measure of the level of new skills that are being used, a measure of how much career development has taken place with the trainee's (this includes advancement as a result of the training intervention such as a promotion or a pay raise), a measure of satisfaction or improved attitude, and a measure of new initiatives taken by the trainee as a result of training. Each level of evaluation reviews different types of data and different categories of data.

These five levels consist of:

1. Reaction and Planned Action – At this level of evaluation measurement is taken of the reaction of the participants and an outline is developed for a plan to use what is learned back in the work place. Usually at this first level of evaluation the trainee may fill out a questionnaire, attitude survey, and or participant feedback.

2. Learning From the Training – Learning objectives should be set that relate back to the usage of those skills. Any training should support the learning objectives and the trainee would be measured with some type of test or evaluation on how much was learned. There are multiple ways to test trainees. The trainees may be compared to other participants or there may be a comparison to a specific criterion. Tests can also take the form of measuring performance of what was taught during the training session; this can also take on the form of simulating real activity that

would take place back in the work setting. Trainees can be measured by self assessment, by performing specific activities, or even assessed by the instructor.

3. Application – For transfer of training to take place the trainee must transfer what was learned to the work place. Questionnaires and surveys are typically the methods of evaluation at this step. Another method of evaluation can be through interviews either by the instructor, management, or even an outside company. Application is activity and activity can also be monitored. A person can view the activities of the trainees to determine if they use the new skills or knowledge. Some of these data collection methods in step three can also apply to data collection in step four.

4. Impact – Impact measures the change that took place by the use of the application of the new knowledge or skills learned by the trainee. Not all application can result in positive impact. The impact of the application from the new knowledge would be measured.

5. ROI – Return on investment is the final step in the Phillips ROI model. ROI takes into account the impact that took

place in level four and quantifies that into some type of return on the investment in training intervention. The general formula for ROI is either Cost/Benefit Ration (CBR) or the ROI formula. CBR is measured as the program benefits divided by the program costs. The results of this equation are in the form of a proportion. The calculation of ROI is the net program benefits (benefits – program costs) divided by the program costs multiplied by 100. The results of measuring using this equation are a percentage.

Alternatives

Formative vs. Summative

Considering Phillips ROI model and its growth from Kirkpatrick's model, it is apparent that the ROI model is effective after training takes place and is not designed for evaluation prior to the training and that may also have had an impact on the training evaluation.

There is a six step transfer model that Stolovitch proposes, though not an evaluation model, it does exemplify the need for formative evaluation along with summative evaluation.[32] Phillips ROI model is rather summative (measurement taken during and after but not before) where a transfer of training program may find better use of a summative and formative evaluation process. Two HRD evaluation models that are both summative and formative are Galvin's CIPP model and Brinkerhoff's six step evaluation model.[33]

CIPP Model

It was from studies in the field of education from which the CIPP model was suggested by Galvin. CIPP means: Context, Input, Process, and Product. Where this model becomes formative is that the context, input, and possibly part of the process are evaluations prior to the actually training. Input can happen before (as training activity is planned) or after training has occurred (reaction) and could be considered summative or formative.

[32] Stolovitch, H. D. (2004). Human performance technology: Research and theory to practice. In R. Chevalier (Ed.), *Human performance technology revisited* (pp. 1-10). Silver Spring, MD: ISPI.

[33] Galvin, J. C. (1983). What trainers can learn from educators about evaluating management training. *Training and Development Journal*, 37(8), 52-57.
33. Brinkerhoff, R. O. (1987). *Achieving results from training.* San Francisco: Jossey-Bass.

To experience a valuable transfer of training process, a needs assessment should be required to ensure that training is necessary. Once a needs assessment is completed a training needs assessment could take place that helps establish the training needs. It is this analysis and the context of the required training that are part of the context portion of the CIPP evaluation model.

The evaluation of input refers to resources. Should internal or external resources be used? What type of strategy will be used? There are also resources such as the training budget, materials, schedules, medium, and other contextual resources.[34] Once the training program is designed and ready for implementation it goes through the process of training. Evaluation can take place throughout this process and is feedback to the trainers. It is this level that closely resembles level one of the Phillips ROI model. The final evaluation is of the product itself. Levels two, three, four, and five of Phillips model could be construed as the measurement of the objectives of the product; which was the training.

---

[34] Morrison, G. R., Ross, S. M., & Kemp, J. E. (2004). *Designing effective instruction*. (4th ed.).

The CIPP evaluation model includes (allows) within its framework the Phillips ROI model. The apparent difference between Phillips ROI model and the CIPP is the formative part of the evaluation. The CIPP model starts the evaluation portion prior to training and allows for evaluation throughout the entire process and summative to measure the results. This does not indicate a lack in the Phillips ROI model, but rather a difference of focus; a difference of type of evaluation of focus and in scope.

Brinkerhoff Model

Brinkerhoff offered a six step evaluation model. This six step process is also a summative and formative evaluation model. Brinkerhoff [35] states "Yet there are many reasons to be concerned with evaluating HRD programs as they happen, well before they have a chance to produce results." The evaluation starts with a specific need. A process that can be used may be a performance analysis or this can be accomplished through some needs assessment and once a gap is found that requires a knowledge intervention, a goal is set. The second step is designing the program. Evaluation needs to take place to determine what needs

---

[35] Brinkerhoff, R. O. (1988). An integrated evaluation model for HRD. *Training and Development Journal, 42*(2), 66-68. P. 66

to take place that will close that gap. What must be accomplished to meet the goal defined by the needs assessment? Different alternatives and solutions may be reviewed at this stage. The third step in the model is the implementation of the program. What is working, what is not? Did the training accomplish that which it was intended for? This third step could include the first level of Phillips ROI model.

The fourth step in the evaluation process is similar to step two of Phillips ROI model, that of measuring learning. The fifth step is where the evaluation of transfer takes place. This is similar to step three of Phillips ROI model. And the final step of Brinkerhoff's six step evaluation model can include levels four and five of Phillips ROI model. Step six is where the measurement of impact is, was the intervention worth it?

Usefulness of the Phillips ROI Model to the Transfer of Training

As a summation of the different transfer of training models, Stolovitch compiled a six step transfer model. The six steps of the model are: Selection, Preparation, Design/Delivery, Support, Feedback, and Incentive/Consequences. Within a Kaizen process where specific tools and methods such as Six Sigma are taught to trainees, it is critical to ensure that transfer takes place back to the work place. It is critical that the correct participants are chosen, that supervision is involved in goal setting for the outcome of the training, that the training and delivery are designed to enhance transfer, that after the training the supervisor offers support, feedback, and that the trainee understands the incentives and or consequences of not meeting the transfer goals. All being said, does the Phillips ROI model suffice as an evaluation for the transfer of training within a Kaizen process?

One of the criticisms of Kirkpatrick's four level evaluation model, of which Phillips ROI model is built from, is that the four step model is summative and not formative. The criticism is that the model only evaluates after the training takes place and does not evaluate any information prior to the reaction to training.[36] Is it always imperative that training evaluation be formative or evaluates prior to training? If it is imperative that the only good evaluation model is one that starts prior to training, then the Phillips ROI model is not a good model. Is it imperative that a training evaluation model

---

[36] Brinkerhoff, R. O. (1988). An integrated evaluation model for HRD. *Training and Development Journal*, *42*(2), 66-68.

evaluate prior to training? If it is not imperative, then possibly the Phillips ROI model stands a chance from the critics.

Another Model

Kaizen is part of performance improvement. Performance improvement can actually be an umbrella where Kaizen exists. Performance Improvement covers any and all improvement initiatives within an organization. It is common for members of ASTD (American Society of Training and Development) and ISPI (International Society of Performance Improvement) to use the ADDIE model.

The ADDIE model is designed to cover the full spectrum from analysis to evaluation. The first three steps in the ADDIE model are: Analyze, Design, and Develop. The last step in the ADDIE model is Evaluate. The evaluation in the ADDIE model is not only summative but can be done throughout the entire performance improvement process. What is left is the 'I' in the model. The 'I' is implementation. Using training as a method to deliver knowledge, skills, and abilities is within the implementation phase of the ADDIE model.[37] Phillips ROI model for evaluation of training would then be within the context of implementation and evaluation of the ADDIE model. If Phillips ROI model contextually exists as part of the implementation and evaluation portion of the ADDIE model, than there is no need to require that the Phillips ROI model un-contextualize and cover the full ADDIE process. The CIPP model and Brinkerhoff training evaluation model were designed to contextually support the full ADDIE spectrum while the Phillips ROI model was not.

If the transfer of training within the Kaizen process is within the context of the implementation of the ADDIE model, then of the three models, only the Phillips ROI model is consistent as a tool for evaluating transfer of training. So, is the transfer of training within the Kaizen process within the context of the implementation portion of the ADDIE model? Well, most of it. If evaluation for the transfer of training is being reviewed for use of an appropriate model of evaluation, then it must be conceded that there is an area that is outside the implementation portion of the ADDIE model.

---

[37] Wilmoth, F. S., Prigmore, C., & Bray, M. (2004). HPT Models: An overview of the major models in the field. In R. Chevalier (Ed.), *Human performance technology revisited* (pp. 28-36). Silver Spring, MD: ISPI.

Transfer of Training

Transfer of training starts with the selection and the design of the training. According to the Stolovitch six step transfer model, the right people need to be chosen for training, the supervisor and employee must have objectives and goals prior to training, and the training design and delivery must support a transfer of training process. Where does the selection of the right individual fall in the ADDIE model? It seems that it falls in the analysis portion of the ADDIE model. An analysis of the ability of the potential trainee must take place and that would take place prior to training. If the supervisor and employee are to set goals for transfer, where does that take place? It also seems to take place at the analysis-development phase of the ADDIE model.

The design and development of the training session so that transfer of training is part of the training design and delivery takes place in the development and design portion of the ADDIE model. It seems that the Phillips ROI model is an excellent model for evaluating if the transfer of training takes place, but it is not a valid model for evaluating the development of the transfer model for a continuous improvement project.

CIPP or the Six Step Evaluation Model

Because it is necessary to evaluate the usefulness of a transfer of training method in a Kaizen process, it is necessary to include steps from either/or the CIPP or six step evaluation model. It has been noted that both the CIPP and the six step evaluation model have steps that allow for the insertion of Phillips ROI model. The CIPP and the six step evaluation models are contextual and allow for variation within each step or category. Steps three through six of Brinkerhoff's six step evaluation model allow for evaluation methods that are similar to the full Phillips ROI model. The process and product area of Galvin's CIPP model allow for the evaluation methods that are similar to the full Phillips ROI model. Given that the Phillips ROI model can fit into either the CIPP or the six step evaluation model, a choice needs to be made as to which model could be used.

It is critical to build partnerships and rally an organization around the Kaizen process. Of the different models suggested what model would be best to facilitate that partnership and organizational rallying? What model would best integrate Phillips ROI model into it?

The Phillips ROI model has five levels and the CIPP model has four levels. These two have a better design fit than a six stage evaluation process. The ADDIE model is also a contextual model that is not staged but follows more of a levels process. Also, the ADDIE model, the CIPP model, and the ROI model are contextual in that each level acts as a fence for activity while Brinkerhoff's six stage evaluation model is more definite in nature in that it sets goals. Therefore, because either the CIPP or the six stage evaluation model can allow for Phillips ROI model to exist as a part of the contextual levels, the choice for the model for presentation will be the contextual of the two, which is the CIPP model with Phillips ROI model used at levels process and product.

Conclusion if Transfer of Training Models

Each organization will have to decide for themselves what models of transfer they will use when they perform Continuous Improvement training. Each organization will have to decide for themselves what models of training evaluation they will use when they perform Continuous Improvement training. The point of this chapter is to remind the organization that Kaizen always includes training and training should always include a transfer model, because training does not change behavior, it only gives information. An organization is not in the business to train people; they are in the business to turn inputs into outputs. This happens through people and processes, those people need to behave in specific ways to turn those inputs into outputs. This means that an organization should only be concerned with guiding the behavior of their human capital. Training does not guide behavior, transfer of training guides behavior. If an organization simply trains their employees and then sends the employee out into the work area without a transfer plan, then that business is in the business of training, and not input to output transfer.

It is also imperative that an organization measures the value of the training and then the subsequent transfer cost against the gains of the changed behavior. If it costs $5 million dollars to implement a full Kaizen culture and the return is only $2 million dollars, is it worth it? The name of the game is turning inputs to outputs where the final output has more value than the inputs. Business seems to be the only place where the second law of thermodynamics does not work!!

Even though this book is not about the transfer of training, it is about Kaizen, Self-Actualization, and Meta-Coaching. The book started with an overview of Kaizen, it was followed by theories of motivation because the idea of Kaizen includes the idea of employee involvement. And finally, the idea of transfer of Kaizen back to the organization, as measured by return on investment, is crucial as one considers using Kaizen as a competitive advantage.

Given that people are motivated by different things and in different ways, and given that there needs to be an intention of transfer of Kaizen back into the organization, the next function in the process is naturally the idea of Self-Actualization; which is the actualizing of one's best and highest. A Self-Actualized individual in a Self-Actualized organization becomes Kaizen in the flesh!

Chapter Four

Self-Actualization

What is Self-Actualization? What does Self-Actualization have to do with Kaizen? Self-Actualization is a psychology and biology. Self-Actualization is the process of becoming. For the individual and for the organization it is the becoming into that which brings potentiality into actuality. It is the making real that which is only felt. Self-Actualization is moving from what one can be to the process of becoming that which one can be.

Self-Actualization is a process. Self-Actualization is not a static event or a goal that is to be met. Self-Actualization is the word or the phrase for the process that individuals, businesses, families, cultures etc. go through as they make what is potential into actual. Self-Actualization is an ongoing process that never needs to end. Self-Actualization is Kaizen.

Now by calling Self-Actualization Kaizen does not mean that Self-Actualizing is about continuously improving oneself, because a person or organization can continually work to improve themselves but that is not necessarily Self-Actualization. Self-Actualization carries with it certain characteristics that are shared by individuals and organizations, characteristics that have come about through a type of Kaizen lifestyle, but that is independent and even a gestalt stage of the Kaizen lifestyle.

Self-Actualization has been defined and studied by different people at different times in recent history. It is a critical part of this study to write about some of this history and to write about why Self-Actualization is necessary for a Kaizen organization. It is also important to point out that Self-Actualization is not some religious or mystical experience by rather a growing up and growing out of the individual. Self-Actualization is the end, through various means, to a person and organization reaching peak experiences, peak performances, truly Kaizen.

What have others said about Self-Actualization? Who are the main theorists, psychologists, and humanitarians who study and write about self-actualization? What are the characteristics of self-actualization? This chapter is broken down into two parts. The first part covers the who's who in self-actualization research and the characteristics of self-actualization. The second part of the chapter discusses the current findings about how self-actualization actually influences business leaders.

Maslow and Self-Actualization

Abraham Maslow recognized that the needs of physical existence, safety, social, and esteem were deficiency needs. People are motivated to fill those needs and thereby reduce the need by fulfillment. When there is a deficiency of food, one seeks food. Once the food is acquired, the need is fulfilled and the person is no longer motivated to change behavior for food. Not all needs are deficiency needs, some needs are growth needs, and Maslow recognized these needs to grow as self-actualization needs. The need for self-actualization is not a deficiency need. It is a need that once fulfilled; the person seeks for even greater fulfillment. It was this need, this self-actualization need that engendered Maslow to state "What humans can be, they must be."[38] What research or experience did Maslow encounter that inspired him to develop such a premise and what forces of psychology or forces in nature

---

[38] Maslow, A. H. (1970). *Motivation and personality*. (3rd. ed.). New York: Harper and Row. p. 22

played a role in developing a life dedicated to stating such a premise and then consequently setting out to measure, define, and develop such a premise in people, in leaders?

Around the time that Maslow began his career there were only a few major forces within the field of psychology; there was the experimental behavioral approach that studied stimulus and response. There was also the psychoanalytic approach that studied the weak and unhealthy side of human nature. Maslow did not believe that these two approaches were sufficient to use for understanding people. Maslow believed that these approaches "sold human nature short" and only looked at the sick side of human nature and did not study the healthy side of human nature.

Around the time that Maslow approached the idea of self-actualization, there was a Third Force within psychology, that force was called the humanistic movement, and it was within this movement that Maslow focused his attention and within this movement that he sought to develop his ideas, his theories, and the implications that came with them.

There were two key people that Maslow interacted with that created a *Weltanschauung* for him. One was Ruth Benedict and the other was Max Wertheimer; both were his teachers after he came to New York City with his Ph.D. Maslow claimed that "they were the most remarkable people." [39] Maslow claimed that in starting to view these two people as remarkable people, he realized that his "investigation began as a prescientific or nonscientific activity." [40] It was from these two people, people who did not fit into the model of brokenness that he learned from his psychological training that his new *Weltanschauung* began to develop. So the beginnings for Maslow were not from a sample of a selected population, but were from him selecting specific individuals in which to research, special individuals who had the qualities of remarkable people.

From these two people Maslow began to study other people, he began to operationalize his terms and define the types of specimens that he would use to study self-actualization. Maslow began to study historical persons and he also began to have confirmatory lines of evidence coming from others, such as Rogers

---

[39] Maslow, A. H. (1971). *The farther reaches of human nature*. New York: Penguin Group. p .40
[40] Maslow, A. H. (1971). *The farther reaches of human nature*. New York: Penguin Group. p. 40

and Bugental. Maslow's research was grounded in sampling the types of people that resembled those he had already studied. In fact, Maslow writes, "If we want to answer the question how tall can the human species grow, then obviously it is well to pick out the ones who are already tallest and study them."[41]

The grand shifting paradigm that fueled the premise of a new view of human nature and the need for humans to self-actualize can be summed up by Maslow.

> but one thing I have no doubt: When you select out for careful study very fine and healthy people, strong people, creative people, saintly people, sagacious people – in fact, exactly the kind of people I picked out – then you get a different view of mankind. You are asking how tall can people grow, what can a human being become? [42]

The need for humans to become what they can become may have started from a view or connotative aspectual framework for Maslow, but it did not stop there. It was not just his research of

---

[41] Maslow, A. H. (1971). *The farther reaches of human nature.* New York: Penguin Group. p.6

[42] Maslow, A. H. (1971). *The farther reaches of human nature.* New York: Penguin Group. p. 42

certain individuals, both in history and through history, but Maslow's understanding of biology, and the drives applicable to biological beings.

Biology has much to teach about the self-actualization of individuals. Maslow states that, "The organism has more tendency toward choosing health, growth, biological success than we would have thought a century ago." [43] Maslow made such a statement because there were other areas of research that were being done on human nature. "Contemporary researchers suggest that the organism is more trustworthy, more self-protecting, self-directing, and self-governing than it is usually given credit for." [44]

The research and debates of biological growth toward self-actualization happened in the framework of human instincts. How strong were human instincts? Do they govern the organism and thus govern the behavior, or are the instincts limited and the human becomes through the process of being? Maslow came to the conclusion that even though humans have some instincts, they

---

[43] Maslow, A. H. (1971). *The farther reaches of human nature*. New York: Penguin Group. P 13
Maslow, A. H. (1970). *Motivation and personality*. (3rd. ed.). New York: Harper and Row., p.46

become fully human by being and experiencing and willing; he stated that the human had "instinctoids."

Maslow believed that humans have this great potential as shown in biological necessity toward growth, but that something blocks their growth. He believed that through a natural process people tend toward growth and not stagnation, yet something blocks them. We have, all of us, an impulse to improve ourselves, an impulse toward actualizing more of our potentialities, toward self-actualization, or full humanness, or human fulfillment, or whatever you like. Granted this, then what holds us up? What blocks us?

But there is danger to the organism to allow this something to block self-actualization; something that blocks the movement of the being to full development and full functionality. This blocking can have many negative effects on one's being and one's experience of that being in this world, it is that revelation that Maslow captured when he wrote, "If you deliberately plan to be less than you are capable of being, then I warn you that you'll be deeply unhappy for the rest of your life. You will be evading your own capacities, your own abilities."[45]

Maslow's Motive

Before moving on toward a finer granulated definition of the process of self-actualization, it is imperative to define further the drive and motive of Maslow. What impetuous drove the life-long research and pursuit of this self-actualization and the full being of the human for Maslow? Maslow saw two great problems that must be solved. The first and foremost big problem was to "make the good person." Maslow was greatly affected by the happenings of World War II and the atomic age. Maslow believed that if humans cannot find a way to make the good person, they may all be wiped off of the face of the earth. Maslow, at the point of determination that humans must develop and have the good person, they must, of course, be able to define the good person. Maslow went on to set a standard of definition of the good person, a person who, according to Maslow, if they could exist in abundance within a good

---

[45] Maslow, A. H. (1971). *The farther reaches of human nature.* New York: Penguin Group. p. 35

society, they may save the race from being wiped of the earth through war.

The second big problem according to Maslow was in developing this good society of good people. Maslow seriously believed that technologies and biological improvements must be put within the hands of good men in good societies. This desire to see and experience good men (and women) within a good society impacted the work and self-actualizing of Maslow and is part of the impetuous of humans becoming fully human.

Self-Actualization

Once Maslow determined that the world needed good people in a good society and that there were good people that could fit into a good society, he had to define what a good person is. What terms, what characters, what traits, would make up a self-actualized person? Were there common traits that these good people shared? Maslow believed that there were at least eight ways in which a person experienced self-actualization.

1. Having moments of total absorption. Being fully focused in whatever activity that one is in. This is experiencing life in time without being self-aware – it is just being. It is a process of being totally focused and absorbed in the moment.

2. Life is a process of choices and the person who is self-actualizing moves from a position of choice from fear choice toward growth choice. It is continuous growth, one step at a time. It is moving forward in life, away from things that engender fear toward things that bring growth.

3. Self-actualizing people are directed by their inner self rather than others. They are the Supreme Court and CEO of their actions and behaviors.

4. Responsibility and truth. Self-actualizing people take responsibility for their actions and their life; they see their life as their responsibility to run and not someone else's.

5. Self-actualizing people grow from making the correct choices at prime times in their life. Self actualizing people live a life of learning how to become what one is. These self-actualizing principles become the foundation for growth and each time they are made the person becomes more

actualized. It is by following their own inner being that they fully become because

6. Self-actualization is an ongoing process and those who are self-actualizing do so with intention and effort. The person who is self-actualizing strives to do their best at what they do.

7. Self-actualizing people experiences key peak experiences, they have times of personal ecstasy. Self-actualizing people finds ways and make avenues to experience peak experiences.

8. Self-actualizing people are on a road to self discovery. They are in process of find themselves, as an existential experience.

Maslow had a further list that could be used for clinical and experimental study: perception of reality, acceptance, spontaneity, problem centering, solitude, autonomy, fresh appreciation, peak experience, human kinship, humility and respect, interpersonal relationships, ethics, means and ends, humor, creativity, resistance to enculturation, imperfections, values, and resolutions of dichotomies. [46]

From these lists and from the research that Maslow did there can be a summation of what all these characters mean for the person, for the self-actualizing person. Maslow compared self-actualizing people as similar to children when he wrote, "Healthy growing infants and children don't live for the sake of far goals or for the distant future, they are too busy enjoying themselves and spontaneously living for the moment. They are living, not preparing to live." [47] Self-actualizing individuals live in the present rather than the past or the future and draw on their own inner resources instead of needing resources from others.

Maslow, though being one of the early researchers and writers about self-actualization, was by no means the only person to research and write about the idea of self-actualizing people. Others have seen common themes of people, who live a life of inner and

---

[46] Maslow, A. H. (1970). *Motivation and personality*. (3rd. ed.). New York: Harper and Row p. 128

[47] Maslow, A.H. (1968/1999). *Toward a psychology of being*. (3rd. Ed). New York: John Wiley & Sons, Inc. p. 53

outer freedom, increase in the utilization of their own capacities, and are less apt to suffer from emotional trauma.[48]

It should be noted that the literature on self-actualization implies in great detail that self-actualization is a process and not a static event. A person does not self-actualize, but rather is always in the process of actualizing, in the process of development.[49] Self-actualization is a process and the individual self-actualizing is not the end in a process, but is the process itself.[50]

Rogers and Others

Rogers was another who saw within the human being the potential to grow and to self-actualization. The more time Rogers spent working and living with people in his person-centered approach, the more he realized that there is a tendency in individuals and

---

[48] Rogers, C. (1961). *On becoming a person*. Boston: Houghton Mifflin Company. 48. Shostrom, E. L. (1962). *Personal orientation inventory*. San Diego CA: Educational & Industrial Testing Service.

[49] Leclerc, G., Lefrancois, R., Dube, M., Hebert, R., & Gaulin, P. (1998). The self-actualization concept: A content validation. *Journal of Social Behavior and Personality*, 13(1), 69-84.

[50] Harre, R. & Lamb, R. (1983). The encyclopedic dictionary of psychology. In Leclerc et al. *Journal of Social Behavior and Personality*, 13(1), 69-84.

groups toward actualization, and that this actualization was a characteristic of life itself.[51]

Rogers believed that in every person there is a current and flow of growth that brings that individual to greater and greater fulfillment of their inherent possibilities. That growth is a process of life and that this process has an inherit base within each individual, and that given the possibility and the reduction of disease or ill-health, the individual moves from a present condition toward a future condition of growth.

Rogers believed that part of his justification for believing that each individual has a tendency to grow toward wholeness and to actualize their potential is that when he used his person centered approach to move people toward growth. He states, "I have not found psychotherapy or group experience effective when I have tried to create in another individual something that is not already there." [52] According to Rogers, the therapist does not create within the individual something that does not already exist in the

---

[51] Rogers, C. R. (1980). *A way of being*. Boston: Houghton Mifflin Company
[52] Rogers, C. R. (1980). *A way of being*. Boston: Houghton Mifflin Company
    p. 120

individual, rather the psychotherapist creates the opportunity for the individual to unleash and grow what is already existent within the individual.

Ellis believed that people have within themselves the drive to achieve a more functional life. Life should be one of discovery of finding what one likes and dislikes, what one can achieve and attain. It should be a process of will of choice to move in the direction of growth by finding out whom and what one is. It is in response to the process of growth and discovery that one begins on the path of self-actualization.[53]

Self-actualization can also go by other names. Others have called self-actualization peak experiences, peak performance, and flow. Privette defines peak experience as intense joy; peak performance as superior functioning; and flow as intrinsically rewarding experience.[54] Maslow recognized self-actualization as including

---

[53] Ellis, A. (1991). Achieving self-actualization. Rational emotive approach. In A. Jones & R.

[54] Privette, G. (1983). Peak experience, peak performance, and flow: A comparative analysis of positive human experiences. *Journal of Personality and Social Psychology,* 45(6), 1361-1368.

peak experiences. These were experiences that surpassed normal levels of experience and were levels of high intensity; these were levels that were rich in meaning. Leach gave a definition of a peak experience as:

> that highly valued experience which is characterized by such intensity of perception, depth of feeling, or sense of profound significance as to cause it to stand out, in the subjects mind, in more or less permanent contrast to experiences that surround it in time and space. [55]

Laski used questionnaires and interviews to collect data from individuals as they reflected in an introspective manner and found that peak experiences could be "characterized by being joyful, transitory, unexpected, rare, valued, and extraordinary to the point of often seeming as if derived from a preternatural source." [56]

Peak performance is that type of behavior that goes above the norm for behavior. Privette states that peak performance was

---

[55] Leach, D. (1962). Meaning and correlates of peak experience. (Doctoral dissertation, University of Florida, 1962).Dissertation abstracts, 1963, 24, 180. (University Microfilms No. 63-0264) p. 11

[56] Laski, M. (1962). *Ecstasy: A study of some secular and religious experiences*. Bloomington: Indiana University Press p. 5

defined operationally as, "behavior which exceeds typical behavior.[57] Privette also states that peak performance may be something that only happens once in a lifetime or it may be something that can happen more often. Peak performance is being on the top of your game. An interesting key point that Thornton, Privette, and Bundrick make about peak performance and its relationship to potential of growth and self-actualization is that, "Evidence that many people experience transient superior performance suggest that humans universally have potential beyond what is ordinarily used." [58]

Flow, as defined by Csikszentmihalyi, is a state of enjoyment, as usually found in play, yet it does not only exist in play.[59] Flow can happen with simple to complex behavior. The key to flow is to have your skill and the challenge of those skills in line with each other. When your skills are matched with the challenge of the job, then you will tend to experience a greater chance to experience flow.

[57] Privette, G. (1983). Peak experience, peak performance, and flow: A comparative analysis of positive human experiences. *Journal of Personality and Social Psychology,* 45(6), 1361-1368.

[58] Thonton, F., Privette, G, & Bundrick, C. M. (1999). Peak performance of business leaders: An experience parallel to self-actualization theory. *Journal of Business and Psychology,* 14(2), 253-264. p. 254

[59] Csikszentmihali, M. (1975). *Beyond boredom and anxiety.* San Francisco: Jossey-Bass

When your skills are greater than your challenges you may experience boredom. When your challenge is greater than your skill you may experience anxiety and fear; flow is that place where there is a match between your skills and your challenges. One may experience a peak experience and not experience peak performance or flow; each is an independent experience that can happen separate or together, yet neither is the antecedent of the other.

Shostrom wrote much about self-actualization, and even developed a therapy to help others self-actualize. Shostrom believed that "the journey of therapy, and of life itself, is from dependence to independence, to interdependence." [60] "But living is a process of continuous change. Therapy, therefore, must be a process of helping man to continuously adapt and change. Research into the affects of actualizing therapy shows that man's core can be revitalized." [61] Self-actualization is becoming who one is, by shaking off that which hinders one from being. It is the process of revitalization and removing of the dross rather than an adding of

[60] Shostrom, E. (1976). *Personal orientation inventory: Manual.* San Diego: Edits p. xxvl

[61] Shostrom, E. (1976). *Personal orientation inventory: Manual.* San Diego: Edits p. 1

attributes or characters. It is growing into full humanness; it is actualizing all of one's potentials, step by step.

Shostrom believed that each person knows who he or she is on the inside, and it is the goal of the self-actualizer to be on the outside what indeed he or she knows to be true of them on the inside. The person needs both to live in homeostasis and in transtasis; change, a transition from one level of homeostasis to another level. A growth toward habituation of what one is on the inside, yet, the self-actualizing individual does not stay in that habitual or homeostatic place but moves and changes toward self determined growth.

Shostrom lists two major and ten minor characteristics of self-actualizing people.

1. Time Competence – Lives in the present
2. Inner Directed – Independent, self supportive
3. Self Actualizing Value – Holds values of self actualizing people
4. Existentiality – Flexible in application of values
5. Feeling Reactivity – Sensitive to own needs and feelings

6. Spontaneity – Freely expresses feelings behaviorally

7. Self-Regard – Has high self-worth

8. Self-Acceptance – Accepting of self in spite of weaknesses

9. Nature of Man, Constructive – Sees man as essentially good

10. Synergy – Sees opposites of life as meaningfully related

11. Acceptance of Aggression – Accepts feelings of anger or aggression

12. Capacity for Intimate Contact – Has warm interpersonal relationships

Campbell , president of Performance Unlimited, seeks to actualize individuals, teams, and organizations.[62] Campbell, taking the lead from Maslow lists most of the same 16 characteristics of actualizing people as does Maslow. Stevens also develops a list of predicates that explain the key characteristics that individuals who experience self-actualization share.[63]

The Center for Self-Actualization gives an interesting definition of the self actualized person.

---

[62] Campbell, J. (1998). Self-actualization. Retrieved from www.performance-unlimited.com/samain.htm

[63] Stevens, T, G, (2005). *Self-actualization*. Retrieved from www.csulb.edu/-tstevens/h12maslo.htm

Seeks to be a 'way shower', cannot settle for mediocrity, always strives to reach greater plateaus, is self contemplative, and seeks to know even the mind's shadows, doesn't readily surrender to fear, sees the means as important conquest, not the end. For the self-actualized there is no end, just a constant movement to expand and become and express more of Oneself![64]

After some discussion of Maslow and his views and contributions toward the idea of self-actualization, the Center for Self-Actualization asks the perspicacious question: "So, what is Self-actualization?" With this question they add further dimension than was stated earlier:

Self-actualization is using your full potential. It's fulfillment on all levels; it is having a basic trust and flow with the universe. It is absent from blockage, such as fear and worry. It is absent of limiting thought, beliefs and prejudices; it is being Spiritually Centered, fully self-identified and fulfilled.

---

[64] The center for self-actualization, Inc. (n.d.). *The self-actualized person.* Retrieved from www.selfactualized.org

Yet, one who is self-actualized is far from self-centered, he is supportive of others and serves as a guide to help them in their movement towards self-actualization.

In this full swoop the Center for Self-Actualization sums up most of what others have written. Each researcher and writer of self-actualization that has been discussed this far has points and sub-points and characteristics of what a self-actualizing person is, in process, this quote incorporates those points into a synthetic manner, and yet, it still leaves out many of the other characteristics that a self-actualizing individual may have.

Stevens reviews the history of self-actualization and the role that Maslow had in that history. Stevens highlights the key characteristics that others have highlighted and then goes further to describe what Maslow called the B-values or B-needs (as opposed to the D-values – deficiency or D-needs). The B-values are being values and are sometimes considered meta-values. Stevens states that, "The content of self-actualizing people's thoughts is an extremely important way in which they live on a higher level. [65]

[65] Stevens, T, G, (2005). *Self-actualization*. Retrieved from

87

Stevens highlights that, "Focusing on satisfying these values (instead of focusing on lower values or negatives) is an important factor in why self-actualizing people are happier, more peaceful, and more productive than other people."

O'Conner and Yballe revisit Maslow's Hierarchy by developing brainstorming teams consisting of students. The teams are to list their needs. Once all the needs are written down O'Conner and Yballe take those needs and start organizing them to find that they fit within the overall structure of Maslow's Hierarchy. In pursuit of their research for a "roadmap of human nature.' O'Conner and Yballe request that the students list their core values. The interesting findings of these values are that they fit within the hierarchy, in the category of self-actualization.[66]

The concept of self-actualization is being researched by neuro-science.[67] It is another avenue of research along the lines of self-

---

www.csulb.edu/~tstevens/h12maslo.htm

[66] O'Conner, D., & Yballe, L. (2007). Maslow revisited: Constructing a road map of human nature. *Journal of Management Education*, 31, 738-756 p. 743

[67] Dietich, A. (2004). Neurocognitive mechanisms underlying the experience of flow. *Consciousness and Cognition*, 13, 746-761

67. Rayback, D. (2006). Self-determination and the neurology of mindfulness. *Journal of Humanistic Psychology*, 46, 474-493

actualization and the predicates that define it, such as peak experience, deep concentration, wholeness, time competence etc. have been vindicated as real positive aspects of human development. Ryback, researches mindfulness and neuroscience to measure the affects that mindfulness has on the neurology of individuals who practice mindfulness (similar in nature to peak experience, deep concentration, wholeness, etc.). Ryback, while discussing the findings of Rogers and Maslow concludes that, "what Rogers was doing all along, even in the 1940s, and the other humanistic pioneers in the 1960s and 1970s, before mindfulness became popular and the neurology that's now cutting-edge research. Somehow, humanistic psychology had it right."[68]

A Kaizen culture will start with your executive management and will filter down to the middle managers and then subsequently to the shop floor, it is apropos then that the next part of this chapter is about the effects that self-actualization has on business leaders and about the effects that has on their performance.

---

[68] Rayback, D. (2006). Self-determination and the neurology of mindfulness. *Journal of Humanistic Psychology*, 46, 474-493 p. 489

Leaders and Self-Actualization

Maslow wrote that self-actualizing business leaders were those who loved their jobs and the dichotomy between work and fun does not exist with self-actualizing individuals.[69] Shostrom built upon the work of Maslow and recognized that people who are self-actualizing are more fully functional and utilize their full capacities and their full capabilities.[70] Understanding the impact of a leader on an organization and the experience of self-actualization should take into account what self-actualization is and what it does for the individual. If a person reaches his or her full capabilities and capacities through self-actualization, and if that person is a leader who reached his or her full capacity and capabilities, then not only does the individual experience success as an individual but success in business as well.[71]

Various research projects have supported the claims that there is a relationship between the level of an individual's self-actualization

---

[69] Maslow, A. H. (1971). *The farther reaches of human nature*. New York: Penguin Group.

[70] Shostrom, E. L., & Knapp, R. R. (1966). The relationship of a measure of self-actualization(POI) to a measure of pathology (MMPI) and to therapeutic growth. *American Journal of Psychotherapy, 20*, 193-202.

[71] Dorer, L. H., & Mahoney, M.J. (2006). Self actualization in the corporate hierarchy. *North American Journal of Psychology*, 8(2), 397-409.

as measured by certain instruments such as the personal orientation inventory and to how satisfied they are with their jobs and careers. These recent finding support the idea that Maslow postulated that those who are self-actualizing would be satisfied with their jobs and careers.

Self-Actualization has been called peak experiences or peak performance. "Peak performance, an optimal experience, parallels and is among a person's closest approximation to self-actualization."[72] These experiences "coincide on many points" [73] and that peak performance is "an episode of superior functioning."[74] Maslow recognized that peak performance was an attribute, or at least an emergent property, of self actualization, and that if businesses leaders were themselves experiencing self-

---

[72] Thornton, F., Privette, G, & Bundrick, C. M. (1999). Peak performance of business leaders: An experience parallel to self-actualization theory. *Journal of Business and Psychology,* 14(2), 253-264. p 253

[73] Privette, G. (1983). Peak experience, peak performance, and flow: A comparative analysis of positive human experiences. *Journal of Personality and Social Psychology,* 45(6), 1361-1368. P 1362

[74] Privette, G. (1983). Peak experience, peak performance, and flow: A comparative analysis of positive human experiences. *Journal of Personality and Social Psychology,* 45(6), 1361-1368. P 1361

actualization, than the experience could bring with it an episode of superior functioning.

Csikszentmihalyi studied, taught, and wrote about flow experiences; about experiences of peak performance, about happiness. Having and experiencing peak moments and being in the flow resulted from the "circuitous path that begins with achieving control over the contents of our consciousness."[75]

The importance of flow, the importance of a new psychology that integrates peak experiences, flow, and happiness are critical for survival of the human species.[76] Maslow wrote about self-actualization as a biological necessity of our species, that is, we are wired to self-actualize.[77] Csikszentmihalyi follows through on this concept when he writes "The first point is that we need a new

---

[75] Csikszentmihali, M. (1990). *Flow: The psychology of optimal experience.* New York: Harper & Rowe p 2

[76] Csikszentmihali, M. (2004). What we must accomplish in the coming decades. *Zygon*, 39(2), 359-366

[77] Maslow, A. H. (1970). *Motivation and personality.* (3rd. ed.). New York: Harper and Row

image of what it means to be human. We have been quite schizophrenic as a species about our own identity. [78]

There was a study comparing the self-actualization level of entrepreneurs who had different growth perspectives relative to expansion of their businesses. They called one set of entrepreneurs as craft-oriented and the other as merchandise-oriented. The craft-oriented were considered to be those who were less growth oriented and the merchandise-oriented were more growth oriented in their business dealings. As part of the conclusion of their study they state that, "Thus, there appears to be a relationship between personal characteristics of the man and (a) the type of firm he builds and (b) the growth of this firm."[79] From their use of the POI, as a measurement of different levels of self-actualization, they found that "Merchandising-oriented entrepreneurs have been hypothesized to be more self-actualizing than craft-oriented entrepreneurs."

---

[78] Csikszentmihali, M. (2004). What we must accomplish in the coming decades. *Zygon*, 39(2), 359-366 p. 360

[79] Lesner, M. & Knapp, R.R. (1974). *Self-actualization and entepenurial orientation among small business owners. A validation study of the POI. Educational and Psychological Measurement, 34*, 455-460. p. 459

Another interesting study suggests that self-actualization, along with assurance and intelligence, had a positive impact on the performance of managers. Two different measures were given to Philippine and Hong Kong Chinese participants. These two measures were the Fiedler's Least-Preferred Coworker Scale (LPC), and Ghiselli's Self-Description Inventory Scale (SDI). It was found that the LPC scores were affected by culture, but for the SDI scale, it was found that those who scored high on self-actualization, also represented those as high performing managers.[80]

Maclagan writes about key theorists such as Herzberg, Argyris, and McGregor and reviews their various theories of motivation and recognized that even within the different theories each theorist agreed that motivating employees will improve performance and that self-actualization is part of employee motivation.[81] In fact, Argyris discusses the growth of employees and states the importance of employee's fully expressing their capabilities by

---

[80] Bennette, M. (1977). Testing management theories Cross-Culturally. *Journal of applied psychology, 62(5),* p. 578-581.

[81] Maclagan, P. (2003). Self actualization as a moral concept and the implications for motivation in organizations: A Kantian argument. *Business ethics: A European review,* 12(4), p. 324-332.

writing that "there be a full expression of the individuals present potential and the striving to expand it."[82]

Others have researched the impact that self-actualization has on the collective action of individuals within organizations. Self-actualization is a second-level level of human development and the third is a transcendental life where "human beings are also in the quest of a harmonious relationship with the external world transcending their narcissistic pursuit of personal gains."[83] It is these levels of human development, which if incorporated within the culture of the organization, has a positive impact on the financial performance of an organization.

It is noted that leaders who portrayed a transformational leadership style have a positive effect on their organization. The study was based off of a regression analysis of CEO's who were transformational leaders, who scored higher than the general population in optimism, self-actualization, problem solving, and assertiveness. The conclusions were not that self-actualization

---

[82] Argyris, C. (1964). *Integrating the individual and the organization*. New York: John Wiley. p. 32

[83] Lang, L. (2008). An integral model of collective action in organizations and beyond. *Journal of Business Ethics*, 80, 249-261. p. 253

made them transformational leaders, but that these CEO's, who were transformational leaders, scored higher on self-actualization than the general population.[84]

The works of Maslow were revisited in the area of Eupsychia type of management and links to self-actualization, at least as it is expressed in organizational management, with work place spirituality. It was stated "We use the eupsychian framework to make sense of the empirical findings of a research aimed at showing how some (eupsychian and antieupsychian) leaders' behaviors influence the (eupsychian and antieupsychian) attitudes and behaviors of employees." The findings revealed then when managers displayed aniteupsychian leadership behaviors it engendered antieupsychian behavior from the employee. When the leader displayed eupsychian leadership it engendered eupsyschian behavior.[85]

---

[84] Meredith, C. L. (2007). *The relationship of emotional intellegence and transformational leadership behavior in non-profit executuve leadership*. Doctoral dissertation. Capella University

[85] Rego, A., Cunha, M. P., & Oliveira, M. (2008). Eupsychia revisited: the role of spiritual leaders. *Journal of Humanistic Psychology,* 48, 165-195. p. 167

There are models for successful growth of teachers. They come to the conclusion that the best way to develop a teacher is to turn Maslow's hierarchy upside down and focus on the soul, focus on self-actualization of the teacher, rather than focus on the lower detailed needs of the teacher. They go so far as to claim "If we step back from our focus on schools and look at how any successful organization envisions professional development, it's not a stretch to say that groups who sustain their workers *do* turn Maslow's pyramid upside down." [86]

Professionalism was higher in associate degree nurses when those same nurses reflected or displayed self-actualizing tendencies. "Findings indicate that self—actualization was positively and significantly related to the degree of professionalism."[87]

There is another research project were there was research of the self/inner development of district superintendants and college deans found that self-actualization was a key concept to the impact that leaders had on the institution.

---

[86] Intator, S. M., & Kunzman, r. (2006). Starting with the soul. *Educational Leadership*, 63(6), 38-42. p. 39

[87] Fetzer, S. J. (2003). Professionalism of associate degree nurses: The role of self-actualization. *Nursing Education Perspectives*, 24(3), 139-143. p. 139

Respondents were asked to rate their level of agreement with the following statement as to their opinion regarding the impact of personal changes (inner transformation) of the leader on their institutions: "If there is no transformation inside each of us, all the structural change in the world will have no impact on our institutions." Of the respondents, 82.4% of the superintendents and 59.1% of the deans agreed or strongly agreed with this statement. [88]

And finally, to wrap up this section about self-actualization and its effect on the performance of business leaders, it seems apropos to bring up the concept of adulthood or full humanity. There has been research into the characteristics of what makes a person fully human. A delineation of many different researchers and theorists captures the essence of their theories of full humanity. The conclusion from these various theorists is that, "Without questions, self-actualization in its process, and in its paradox, is essential to being an adult self." [89] Even though this article does not deal with

---

[88] Metzger, C. (2003). Self/inner development of educational administrators: A national study of urban school district superintendants and college deans. *Urban Education*, 38(6), 655-687. p. 673

[89] Shea, J. J. (2003). The adult self: Process and paradox. *Journal of adult development*, 10(1), 23-30 p. 28

leadership, per se, it does delineate the role self-actualization has in the development of the adult self, and subsequently leaders.

This section on Self-Actualization has covered the idea of the importance of self-actualizing leaders. Self-actualization is the making actual of the potential. It does not take a great inductive leap to realize that given self-actualized leaders have a greater impact on organizational performance, self-actualized leaders focused on Kaizen, will have a double impact on performance. Kaizen is to continually grow as an organization, Self-actualization is to grow as a person, Kaizen self-actualization than can be considered, Kaizen squared!

Given that we know a bit about Kaizen, that is, what it is and what it does. And given that we have some ideas of what motivates people to behave and that we have to ensure a transfer of training and a measurement of its success and that self-actualization can have a positive impact on employee behavior, how does one experience and incorporate this experience of reaching their full potential? How can that experience of self-actualization help an organization develop a culture of Kaizen and thereby gaining a competitive advantage over its competitors?

Chapter Five

Society of Neuro-Semantics

Having considered something about self-actualization and its characteristics and its importance to human and organizational development, we next move on to the idea of Meta-Coaching. But, before we move directly into Meta-Coaching, some of the theories of self-actualization that the Meta-Coach holds should be delineated.

Dr. Michael Hall writes extensively about self-actualization in his published books, in journal articles, and as part of his public articles on his website www.neurosemantics.com. Seeing that Hall and Duval write and train Meta-Coaches and that this training includes concepts of self-actualization and has as part of its goals to help the client and the coach self-actualize as a process, it is important that the literature that Hall writes is taken into consideration so as to understand the direction and goals of the Meta-Coach related to Hall's understanding of self-actualization.

101

Hall's interest in self-actualization includes a history of self-actualization, including the people involved, as well as the psychology that surrounds it. After extensive research into how self-actualization is defined by various researchers and practitioners, and after determining the theoretical construct and psychology of such, he sets out to define self-actualization as it relates to the latest finding in Neuro-Linguistic Programming (NLP), Neuro-Semantics (NS), Meta-States, Meta-Programs, and Meta-Coaching.

Hall recognizes that self-actualization was part of the human potential movement and that there are no one group or groups who promote any models for forwarding the human potential movement into the 21st century. Hall recognizes that NLP was one of many groups that came out of the human potential movement. Hall was on a search to "distinguish remedial psychology from generative psychology," [90] to identify the differences between those who needed therapy and those who have the mental health and self-esteem that could use coaching. One of the grand epiphanies that came from this study was that even though the

---

[90] Hall (2003 p. 2

human potential movement studied the health/growth side of human nature, Hall states there were no models (other than Maslow's) that came out of that movement. There were grand ideas, there were ideals of what humans can be and can become, but no models on how to get there.[91]

Giving that, according to Hall, that there is no single group that has carried on the human potential movement, from which we get self-actualization, who could carry it on? Is it to be lost forever? Can it be revitalized by something? Can it be revitalized by a model or models? Hall believes so, he believes that NLP and NS have the models that "can take self-actualization to a whole new level."[92] But, what from the human potential movement would be carried on and revitalized? Hall states, "Pioneers of the human potential movement offered *a new paradigm* about human nature. Key among their most revolutionary ideas are the following, ideas that governed their new approach:"

1. People innately have the resources and drive to grow and fulfill their nature.

---

[91] Hall (2004

[92] Hall (2004 p. 4

2. Self-actualizing is the natural and the ultimate purpose of life.

3. Unlike animals, we don't have hard-wired instincts for knowing how to be human.

4. We have to discover and invent how to live and be by fulfilling our lower and higher needs.

5. People naturally learn and change when interferences are removed and the right environment is provided.

6. Growth through ongoing learning and change is not only natural and innate but our key "instinct" for survival.

7. Pathology is the exception, not the rule, and not the direction of growth but the interference of growth.

8. Trusting the natural process means giving unconditional positive regard. [93]

At this point then, there is open for further review both the concept of self-actualization as defined by Hall and the model or models that can take self-actualization to the new level. Hall considered this new level as "Actualizing Maslow." To actualize Maslow then, according to Hall, "we will need to :

---

[93] (Hall, 2003, pp. 1-2

1. Translate the *vision* of self-actualization into a specific *model.*

2. Re-model the hierarchy of needs to make it more holistic and systemic.

3. Create specific patterns for accessing and managing "peak" experiences.

4. Create a synthesis between meaning and performance." [94]

5.

Hall then goes on to define exactly what he means by self-actualization

> *Self-actualization* refers to "making real or actual" our innate talents, aptitudes, and possibilities to release our highest potentials. We do this by satisfying our lower needs that drive us (i.e., food, water, sleep, etc., safety, love and affection, and self-esteem) and moving into the highest *being* needs by learning, growing, changing, and transforming.[95]

---

[94] Hall, 2003, p. 3
[95] Hall (2003 p.3

Hall generates a table that describes the tasks that need to be done and the solution for each task; it is within this framework that Hall determines how to actualize Maslow.

Figure 2: Actualizing Maslow

<table>
<tr><td colspan="2" align="center">**Actualizing Maslow**</td></tr>
<tr><td colspan="2">To Actualize Maslow and the great promises of the *human potential movement,* we need to—</td></tr>
<tr><td align="center">**The Task**</td><td align="center">**The Solution**</td></tr>
<tr><td>1) Translate the vision of self-actualization into a specific model.</td><td>Neuro-Semantics of Self-Actualization</td></tr>
<tr><td>2) Re-model the hierarchy of needs so that it is more holistic and systemic.</td><td>The Matrix of Self-Actualization</td></tr>
<tr><td>3) Create specific patterns for accessing and managing "peak" experiences</td><td>Accessing Personal Genius Pattern</td></tr>
<tr><td>4) Create a synthesis between meaning and Performance</td><td>The Self-Actualization Quadrants</td></tr>
</table>

Figure 2: Hall's task to solution chart (Hall, 2003, p. 7).

Before going on to the models, and then ultimately to Meta-Coaching as a way to actualize these models it is very important to delineate Hall's view of self-actualization. As has already been stated, Hall is in agreement with Maslow and Rogers in their definitions of self-actualizing people. Hall starts there and moves out to re-define and co-define with Maslow and others. Hall, in particular considers part of self-actualization as being in a genius state or a flow state. Hall states that some of the variables or qualities of genius state are:

1. An intense focus or concentration, the state of "flow"

107

2. Single tracking or first-level attention focus

3. Multiple perspectives that gives one "wisdom" of the whole

4. An engagement or commitment state about something of interest

5. Clean state accessing and impeccable state shifting in and out of the genius state

6. Crystal clarity of purpose and direction

7. A flow state of optimum challenge and competency

8. Congruency and personal alignment with values and beliefs

9. Empowering decisions for the clarity of the focus state

10. A sense of delight, joy, fun, and happiness in the state

11. An engagement that creates a joyful learning state

12. A flexibility of consciousness to take multiple perspectives

13. Proactively involved in an active way in the engagement

14. Socially involved and connected with others as collaborators or colleagues

15. Detailing the specifics from a meta-position, meta-detailing
[96]

Hall states that he is frequently asked do define genius state, of which, his typical reply is,

---

[96] Hall, 2003, p.2

The genius state is a state in which you are totally and completely present to something, so present in fact, that the world goes away, time goes away, self goes away, everything vanishes and you are present with one thing— you are completely engaged and absorbed with one thing which totally captivates your attention. This is a state of flow. It is an altered state of focus. And it's a great state because all of your resources are completely available to you. This is the state that world-class athletes access when they speak about being "in the zone." This is the state that lovers access when they are spell-bound by each other and lost in the moment. This is the state that young mothers and fathers experience with a new baby. This is what we call a state of transcendence, mystery, loving, and beingness. [97]

How do all these varied paraphrases, explanations, and definitions ferret out into a workable model? What model or process or procedure can dare enjoin all these descriptive being emergent processes and operationally incubate them into both the person who seeks to engender these emergent processes into others, and

---

[97] Hall (2003 p. 1

those who receive these emergent processes? Dr. Hall and Master Coach Duval propound that Meta-Coaching can. The Meta-Coach has the experience of intense training, and of an intense dance with the client, as they facilitate and mobilize the clients internal and external resources to meet the desired well formed outcome of which, the client experiences transformation growth; otherwise known as self-actualization.[98]

Meta-Coaching

Why should the Meta-Coach be expected to have or experience self-actualization? The Meta-Coach coaches the client toward self-actualization, "coaching facilitates self-actualizing human potential." [99] Hall states, "Coaching is the self-actualization technology for the twenty-first century that enables people to unleash resources and, by closing the knowing-doing gap, actually actualizing potential." [100]

---

[98] Hall & Duval, 2006)
[99] Hall & Duval, 2004, p. 27
[100] Hall L. M., & Duval, M. (2006). *The international meta-coaching training system.* Clifton, CO: Neuro-Semantic Publications. p. 23

Leading the client toward self-actualization means leading oneself toward self-actualization, because, according to the values of Neuro-Semantics (originators and trainers of Meta-Coaches) is "Apply to self. To walk the talk, reflect on your own development, and lead by going first in self-application." [101] As part of the vision, mission, and values that the new Meta-Coach trainee has to sign, it also states "Being held responsible helps me to bring out my best, my personal genius." [102] Thus, even from the very start of Meta-Coach training the coach is required to believe and live the values of "personal genius."

Duval states, "Coaching seeks to support a clients desire for change and transformation and yet at the same time, the coach will similarly be affected." [103] So it is apparent that the two founders and key trainers of Meta-Coaching believe and train that the Meta-Coach will experience the same transformation as the client.

---

[101] Hall L. M., & Duval, M. (2006). *The international meta-coaching training system.* Clifton, CO: Neuro-Semantic Publications. p 5

[102] Hall L. M., & Duval, M. (2006). *The international meta-coaching training system.* Clifton, CO: Neuro-Semantic Publications p 7

[103] Hall L. M., & Duval, M. (2006). *The international meta-coaching training system.* Clifton, CO: Neuro-Semantic Publications p 26

What gives Hall and Duval such confidence in Meta-Coaching? Is Meta-Coaching supported by any grounded theories? What theoretical foundations explain coaching and the process of coach and client? Hall and Duval state that coaching has its foundation in various different psychological theories and thus has a solid framework from cognitive-behavioral psychology, developmental psychology, self-actualization psychology, group and team psychology, management and leadership psychology, communication psychology, and sports psychology.[104] In fact, Neuro-Semantics garnered patterns of change from Neuro-Linguistic Programming as found in Satir (Family Systems), Perls (Gestalt Psychology), Erickson (Ericksonian Hypnosis), Bateson (cybernetics, anthropology), Korzybski (General Semantics), Milller, Pribram, Galanter, and Chomsky of the cognitive psychology movement.

Therefore, given that there is theory behind what and why Meta-Coaches do what they do, the next depth of review needs to be the models that Hall describes as key toward "dancing" the client from their current state to a state or place of self-actualizing. From

---

[104] Hall, 2004, p. 14

112

Figure 2 Hall lists four tasks for actualizing Maslow, which would emerge a process for actualizing a client, and a coach. According to Hall, there is the task to "translate the vision of self-actualization into a specific model" of which the solution chosen by Hall is "Neuro-Semantics of Self-Actualization".[105]

A second task is to "Re-model the hierarchy of needs so that it is more holistic and systemic" of which the solution chosen by Hall is "The Matrix of Self-Actualization". A third task is "Create specific patterns for accessing and managing 'peak' experiences" of which the solution chosen by Hall is "Accessing Personal Genius Pattern." A fourth task is "Create a synthesis between meaning and performance" of which the solution chosen by Hall is "The Self-Actualization Quadrants."

Task number one is to translate the vision of self-actualization into a specific model and the solution or model is Neuro-Semantics. What is Neuro-Semantics? It is the meaning that one feels in his or her body. The body includes the mind. It is, in fact, the mind-body system. There are multiple definitions of Neuro-Semantics, but the

---

[105] Hall (2003, p. 7)

key is that "Neuro-Semantics is the scientific term for what is commonly called the mind-body connection. It involves a working model of the translation of mental meaning into physiological responses (emotions, behaviors, reactions)."[106] A further definition that clarifies the scientific term as written above is:

> The meanings (semantics) that we have in our minds by means of our words, language, memory, and imagination does not just stay in our heads, it gets into our bodies. Our neurology translates the meanings in our minds into feelings in our bodies (neurology) so that we then experience neuron-semantic states. [107]

Hall and Duval list the framework of Neuro-Semantics and some of the models that describe, develop, and frame meanings into the mind-body-emotional system. These Neuro-Semantic models include the communication model of NLP; these are the mental representations that are the movies played in the head. Hall describes these as "the theater of our mind." [108] Also, part of Neuro-Semantics is the reflexivity model of Meta-States. A Meta-

---

[106] Hall, 2000a, p. 4
[107] Hall, 2000a, p. 4
[108] Hall L. M., & Duval, M. (2006). *The international meta-coaching training system.* Clifton, CO: Neuro-Semantic Publications p. 30

State is "A state about another state as in joyful about learning, playful about being serious, curious about anger, calm about fear." [109]

The Axis of Change is another model that works with generative change. The Axis of Change model is a change model for those people who already have the ego-strength to change. The Axis of Change model is the change model that the Meta-Coach uses to dance with the client through the change process and includes the motivation to change, the decision to change, the co-creation of the change, and the sustainability of the change.

There is also a Benchmarking model that is used to measure the competencies of the Meta-Coach; terms and methods are operationalized by definition and is a way to measure competencies. The Matrix model is another Neuro-Semantic model. "With the Matrix model we can detect, enter, and profile a person's structure of meaning-making and intervene in the mind-body-emotion system for transformation and enrichment." [110] Ultimately, this leads to the understanding that people give

---

[109] Hall, 2000a, p. 3
[110] Hall & Duval, 2006, p. 30

meaning to everything, and that this meaning is semantic, and that semantically the body receives commands and thus behavior follows thought.

Thoughts and language can become metabolized and though it may start as a thought, it may move into the muscle and affect the behavior. Meta-Coaches coach to the body, via the semantics of the client. It is with this understanding and skill that the Meta-Coach can move the client to experience self-actualizing changes.

A second task is to "Re-model the hierarchy of needs so that it is more holistic and systemic" [111] of which the solution chosen by Hall is "The Matrix of Self-Actualization". Maslow's Hierarchy of needs is a linear model with one need being pre-potent to the next. The Matrix of Self-Actualization takes into account systems thinking and pre-supposes that people have psycho-logics and even the lower needs, or deficiency needs, have psychological impulses. The matrix that one lives in consists of process matrices and content matrices. The process matrices have to do with the meanings that one gives to something. Another aspect of process within the

---

[111] Hall, 2003, p. 7

matrix of the mind is the intentional matrix. What does one want? What is the purpose? Being in state is also part of the process matrix. There are also content matrices. Each person develops a meaning or a matrix that runs their lives.

These matrices include the concept of self. This is when one asks – who am I? There is the matrix of power. Asking questions like, what can I do? Should I do it? These are part of the power matrix. There is also the time matrix. How one feels about time is part of that matrix. Is time the enemy or the friend? One's view of others is also part of a matrix of the mind. One's view of who are other people? Are they nice or mean? And finally the final content matrix of the mind is the world matrix. The world matrix is a bit ontological and asks questions about reality – what is life? What is real?

A third task is, "Create specific patterns for accessing and managing 'peak' experiences" of which the solution chosen by Hall is "Accessing Personal Genius Pattern." Accessing personal genius is a training that the Meta-Coaches go through. There are several different patterns of thought and behavior that the Meta-Coaches learn. The patterns are part of a three day training that uses the

Neuro-Linguistic Programming model (NLP), the Meta-States model, and Neuro-Semantics. NLP is a communication model for running your own brain. Hall states,

> We run our own brain by using the languages of the mind, the languages that we use to create our cinemas that we play out on the theater of our mind. These are the sights (visual), sounds (auditory), and sensations (kinesthetics), smells (olfactory) and tastes (gustatory) senses. We make sense of things with our internal senses. We internally process information and represent such in our MovieMind.[112]

Hall claims that if people would stop and pay attention to their communication, there are movies that play in the mind. Hall is not claiming that there are actual movies, but that people can see pictures, hear sounds, feel sensations, etc. Part of running your own brain is having the opportunity to edit and change the movies in the mind, which has the effect of changing the feelings and moods of the individual. [113] In fact, NLP is a communication model

---

[112] Hall (2000a) p. 3
[113] Hall, L. M., & Bodenhamer, B. G. (2005). *The users manual for the brain: Volume II.* Norwalk, CT: Crown House Publishing Co

that enables, through modeling others, the ability to modify one's behavior. NLP will provide "a set of tools that will enable him or her to analyze and incorporate or modify any sequence of behavior that they may observe in another human being." [114] NLP offers a host of interventions that modify behavior by modifying the representational systems.[115]

Another pattern of the Accessing Personal Genius training is the Meta-States model. The Meta-States model has already been referred to earlier in the literature review. Because humans use reflexive thinking and have states about states, the Meta-State model is a key model for the Meta-Coach in working with the coaching client. Recognizing and working with the clients states and their meta-states ensures that the Meta-Coach enters into the clients Matrix and builds rapport with the client and experiences the map of the client, rather than functioning from their own maps.

[114] Dilts, R., Grinder, J., Bandler, R., & Delozier, J. (1980). *Neuro-linguistic programming: Volume1 the study of the structure of subjective experience*. Cupertino, CA: Meta Publications. p 3
[115] Bolstad, R. (2002). *Resolve: A new model of therapy*. Williston, VT: Crown House Publishing

The other model that that the Meta-Coach uses integrates states and meanings through Neuro-Semantics to engender a movement from thought to body, or as Hall calls it "the gap between knowing and doing." Closing that gap is moving what is in the mind into the muscles. The Neuro-Semantic models that are part of the accessing personal genius are the:

1. Meta-States model – maps the reflexivity and describes the layering of states upon states.

2. The Mind-Lines model – this model is for reframing conversations.

3. The Frame Games model – this model looks at the frames that one uses and the games that are played using those frames.

4. The Matrix model – this model specifies the seven different matrices that every person uses. It is a diagnostic model that looks at the matrix of intention, meaning, self, time, power, others, and the world.

5. The Axes of Change model – this model maps the changes that the client goes through starting with their motivation

toward change and ending with validating and sustaining the change.[116]

It is within this framework and models that Accessing Personal Genius training takes place. Each certified Meta-Coach goes through this training and is able to use these models and has patterns that can be used to bring transformational change, self-actualizing change within themselves and their clients. There are fourteen key areas of training that each Meta-Coach goes through that enables them to self-actualize and experience a genius state, as well as prepares them to work with a client to self-actualize and experience a genius state.

1. There is a general introduction to the Meta-States as a model of reflexivity.
2. There is meta-stating awareness and ownership of their basic powers. This highlights the fact that the coach, and the client, has the power to think, feel, behave, and speak. There is a pattern that is followed that the trainee goes through to develop this meta-state.

---

[116] Hall, 2006b, p 4

3. There is the meta-stating of the self for self-acceptance, appreciation, and awe (esteem). There is a pattern that is followed that the trainee goes through to develop this meta-state of self-acceptance, appreciation and awe. The Meta-Coach must have the ego strength and a positive self-regard and self-acceptance as part of self-actualization.[117]

4. There is the meta-stating of thoughts of confirming and disconfirming to commission or to decommission beliefs. This is state ownership of the belief's that the Meta-Coach wants that are resourceful. This is also a pattern that the trainee goes through.

5. There is also a state of pleasure. The art of joy, of delight and happiness. Self-actualization includes the concepts of joy and pleasure and the Meta-Coach learns how to create and enjoy the state of enjoyment.

6. There is a conceptual deprogramming. It is a meta-stating of concepts. This is a pattern of changing the meaning that one can give to a concept. One may have a poor relationship

---

[117] Shostrom, E. L. (1962). *Personal orientation inventory*. San Diego CA: Educational & Industrial Testing Service.

with a concept and that relationship may undermine the ability for the person to experience life to the fullest; another concept of self-actualizing.

7. There is a pattern for taming "dragons". It is a pattern for learning to get rid of toxic thoughts, morbid states, unbalanced states – there may be times when one uses their own energies to put themselves at odd with themselves, these are referred to as dragon states. The trainee learns how to tame these dragons.

8. There is an "as if" frame. This is the miracle frame. It is a pattern that helps elicit and develop states of possibility or miracle thinking.

9. The mind-to muscle pattern is also learned and run. It is a pattern for taking a concept and driving it into behavior. It is a pattern for getting a great idea or concept from the conceptual level to the body level and even to a state of habituation.

10. There is state training and a pattern to develop a state of intentionality. A person may have a state of attention, but they need to move from attention toward intention.

11. The genius state is a state of focus and concentration. This pattern is about state shifting, focus, self trust, commitment, and the ability to get lost in the moment.

12. There is a pattern to blowout excuses that one uses – excuses that hinders one from reaching their fullest potential and self-actualizing.

13. There is a pattern of meta-stating to resolve internal conflicts – it is to become congruent in thoughts and behaviors. It is bringing together miss match into a new whole or gestalt. This is also another level of self-actualization – the synergistic mind.

14. The final pattern is meta-stating integrity. It is the alignment of all ones values with all ones behaviors.[118]

All these patterns and this training help prepare the future Meta-Coach to experience self-actualization and to bring the client to self-actualizing. The Meta-Coach not only uses the patterns for their personal growth and control of states, but has tools and models for actualizing in their clients the client's highest potentials. Thus, it seems, right from the start of the training of the Meta-

---

[118] Hall, 2000, pp. 7-9

Coach that the coach is learning and practicing states that in and of themselves increase the level of self-actualization.

Shostrom, taking his lead from Maslow, in creating the Personal Orientation Inventory (POI), measures multiple dimensions for determining levels of self-actualization. As has already been highlighted earlier in this chapter, Shostrom lists two major and ten minor characteristics of self-actualizing people.[119]

Which, if any, of the Meta-States that are patterned and developed within the APG training would increase the probability that the Meta-Coach would score as a self-actualizing individual? According to Hall, the accessing personal genius involves the 14 meta-states that were just listed of which elicits 21 meta-state experiences. Therefore, there are 21 opportunities to practice the 14 different meta-states. So, with this preliminary training, prior to Meta-Coach training, the trainee has opportunity to move toward self-actualization.

---

[119] Shostrom, E. (n.d.). *POI scales*. Retrieved from www.edits.net/POI-scales.html

Given that we now know what self-actualization is, what it means to the individual and the business leader, and what the Meta-Coach understands about self-actualization, it is now imperative that we look at what the Meta-Coach experiences during their training. The premise of this book is that the Meta-Coach can facilitate the mobilization of your executives, middle manager, and employee's inner resources so they can experience the actuality of the potentiality of a true Kaizen culture. What does the Meta-Coach learn and transfer to behavior that allows for such a credulous expression of sincerity and personal Kaizen?

Chapter Six

Meta-Coaching

How does a person make real that which is potential? Are there models or methods or methods and models that a person uses or can use that would facilitate this self-actualization that so many have written about and that, if captured, would bring about transformational change that would engender a true Kaizen culture?

Meta-Coaching is a process that facilitates the mobilization of a person's resources so as that they can actualize their potentials. Through a fierce conversation, the individual or individuals who are interested in making real that which is at present only a potential, experience transformational change, transformational change that facilitates the Kaizen culture.

It is through the Meta-Coach process that your executives, middle managers, and employee's at all levels of the organization face the opportunity to experience deep lasting self-actualizing changes that are themselves part of the human Kaizen process and ultimately part of the organizations Kaizen experience.

The Meta-Coach goes through a rigorous training, using seven different models from which they are the facilitators of self-actualizing changes. Let us begin the rest of this chapter with covering some of the models and methods through which the Meta-Coach is trained and through which the Meta-Coach is ultimately benchmarked and finally certified as a self-actualizing change agent.

Meta-Coach Training

The Meta-Coach training is eight days long. Each day has a different emphasis but all the days together create a new gestalt – A Meta-Coach. This chapter about the Meta-Coach training will not cover every facet of what is trained on each day, but rather those key concepts that prepare the Meta-Coach to self-actualize and prepare the Meta-Coach to coach your executive, middle manager, and employee into the self-actualization process and the Kaizen culture.

Therefore, some of the training about how to establish a SWOT analysis, develop a business plan etc. will not be covered in this review. This does not mean that the development of the SWOT analysis or the development of a business plan has no affect on the self-actualizing potential for the Meta-Coach, only that other areas have more relevance.

Key Relevant Topics of Day 1:

One of the key topics of day one is the introduction of a change model that Hall and Duval developed called the Axis of Change model. When Hall considered coaching and the theoretical framework of such, he noticed that coaching did not have its own specific change model, but tended to borrow from therapy. Coaching is not therapy but is for those who have the ego-strength to change by their own will and intention.

Hall and Duval developed a change model that followed the process of which a person, who was not being forced to change, changed. The Axis of Change model has four different axes of change. The first axis is the energy axis or the motivational axis. When the Meta-Coach and client are addressing the motivation toward change, the client can either be moving away from something, or moving toward something, or both. The Meta-Coach learns this axis and learns how to recognize if the client's motivation is away from something, or is toward something. The Meta-Coach is brought to an understanding that if the client is moving away from something, like moving away from lost profits because of poor quality and inefficient processes, as the form of motivation, than they can challenge the client with current reality. If the client is motivated toward an object or goal, like leaner processes, more customers, competitive advantage, then the Meta-Coach can awaken the client toward a new vision. The Meta-Coach learns to recognize the energy of the client and thus facilitate that energy toward change.

The Meta-Coach, now with an understanding of motivation as being either toward a goal or object, or away from something, learns how to coach both sides and thus bring a balance to motivation not only in his or her life, but also in the life of the client and can use this meta-program toward his or hers own self-actualization.

Another topic covered in day one is understanding the seven core coaching skill. The Meta-Coach trainee's not only learn what these skills are but are benchmarked against them. Each core skill has a rating of zero to five. Zero being the lowest level that one has in showing the application of that skill and five being at the top of the skill. These core coaching skills are:

1. Listening – The scale of listening at the lowest level is spending more time telling and interrupting the client, rather than listening to the client. The highest scale of listening is listening both for auditory and body language. At the highest level the coach is mostly quite while being totally present with the client.

2. Supporting – This is where the client feels safe with the coach because the coach is managing the coaching environment. The lowest scale of supporting is that the coach is impatient with the client and the highest scale is when the client's agenda and outcomes are the foremost concern and the coaching session is only about the client's growth and needs.

3. Questioning – This coaching skill is geared toward how well the coach can send the client inward to recognize his or her own beliefs, frames, values, ideas, etc. The lowest scale is the coach, instead of asking penetrating questions, advises and tells the client what to do, what to believe, what to value, etc. The highest scale is when the questioning creates forward movement for the client – the questions flow so as to bring the client closer to his or her desired future state or goal.

4. Meta-Questioning – Meta-questioning is asking questions about previous questions. It includes asking about the state of the client, about the feelings in the body, and the emotions in the body. The lowest scale is only enquiring into the primary levels – mostly only asking questions about content and not process. The highest scale is asking questions that are loaded with presuppositions so that they facilitate a change in the world view or a paradigm shift forward for the client.

5. Inducing States – It is important that the Meta-Coach understands and knows how to induce states within the client. This can happen by telling stories, metaphors,

132

inflections in the voice, specific bodily gestures etc. The
lowest scale is to ignore the state of the client or the coach's
state is not congruent with the client's state. The highest
scale is getting the client induced into a state and even
amplifying the state in abundance and then calibrating how
much of the state the client is in.

6. Giving Feedback – The Meta-Coach needs to offer feedback
   to the client both in words and in bodily gestures that
   provide support for the client. The lowest scale is
   withholding any feedback toward the client and the highest
   scale is feedback that is measured and strategic. This is also
   feedback that is not advice or telling but offers reflective
   communications.

7. Receiving Feedback – The Meta-Coach needs to understand
   and have rapport with the client. The Meta-Coach needs to,
   through the use of the other skills, reflect on the
   communication received from the client and developing
   further useful questions that improve the performance of
   the client. The lowest scale is that the coach is disengaged
   from the client. The client may answer the Meta-Coaches
   questions, but the Meta-Coach is not engaged so the

responses are not reflected and fed back with further questions. The highest scale is celebrating the breakthroughs with the client – continuously improving step by step the communication and rapport between the Meta-Coach and the client.

If the Meta-Coach becomes competent with these skills, how does that affect his or her self-actualization? As the Meta-Coach trainee learns these skills and practices these skills and then uses these skills with your executive, middle manager, and employee, then the Meta-Coach trainee has changes in his or her frames, values, perceptions, etc. and change as each client experiences the matrix of their mind and move toward self-actualization. It seems that it would be this movement of the client that would increase the self-actualization of the coach in the same areas as that of the client.

Also in day one the Meta-Coach trainee's learn about the intentionality matrix. The Matrix model has already been introduced in the last chapter and one of the matrices that every person has is intentionality – the will and intention to do or be something. Key to the intentionality matrix is the meaning matrix, the meanings that a person gives to that which they are intentional about. Hall and Duval state, "The Intentional Matrix addresses our sense of direction, goals, reasons, purpose, motivation, and intention."[120] The Meta-Coach learns some questions that can be asked to elicit responses and states from the client about his or her intention matrix. This process of questioning, using the skills of the Meta-Coach, sends the client inward to reflect and find out his or her real intentions. The Meta-Coach can ask questions such as: What do I want? What am I living for? What do I hope to gain from attaining something else? Part of the Meta-Coaches training is that the trainees not only hear a lecture from the trainers, but they see a demonstration with a real client (usually a trainee), and they practice with other trainees; so, the coach experiences this first hand by doing and receiving.

Key Relevant Topics of Day 2:

The key trainings and experiences that take place on day two are an explanation of the Matrix model, an exercise for detecting a person's matrix (the trainee's go through an exercise in

---

[120] Hall L. M., & Duval, M. (2006). *The international meta-coaching training system.* Clifton, CO: Neuro-Semantic Publications p. 125

understanding their own matrix and that of another). The Meta-Coach trainees also learn about the 10 coaching states (or whatever number of states the Meta-Coach create as part of his or her coaching states), states that a coach should be able to put on and take off as needed in the dance with the client. As each model is described and then demonstrated, the Meta-Coach physically practices with others working through these models so they have the opportunity to not only coach the models, but experience the models as a client.

During day two the Meta-Coach trainee is offered a refresher in the Matrix model that they learned and experienced in the APG training. The Matrix model reveals the states that each person has about meaning, intention, self, power, time, other, and the world. Understanding and working with these matrices offers the Meta-Coach trainee a glimpse, even a deep dive, into what is important to them, how they give that importance meaning, and how they view themselves as a person, how they view time, how they view power, how they view others, and how they view the world.

Another aspect of the training in day two is for the Meta-Coaches in training to find their top ten coaching states. This does not all happen in one sitting or on the same day, but the Meta-Coaches in training learn to define their top states for coaching. They learn how to induce the states within themselves and how to turn them off, within themselves. This then becomes a skill for the Meta-Coach in training to experience state management. Having the ability to enter into any state that is best suited for the individual coach ensures that the Meta-Coach in training has the ability to do so.

Also during the training at this stage the Meta-Coach trainees learn about emotion, which, according to Hall, is the difference between a person's map of the world and his or her experience of the world. The Meta-Coach trainee comes to understand this and to accept emotions as neither good nor bad, but as the output of the variance between the map and the experience.

Key Relevant Topics of Day 3:
The third model that the Meta-Coach in training learns and experiences is the Self-Actualization Quadrants. The Self-

Actualization Quadrants is constructed from the meaning/performance axes.

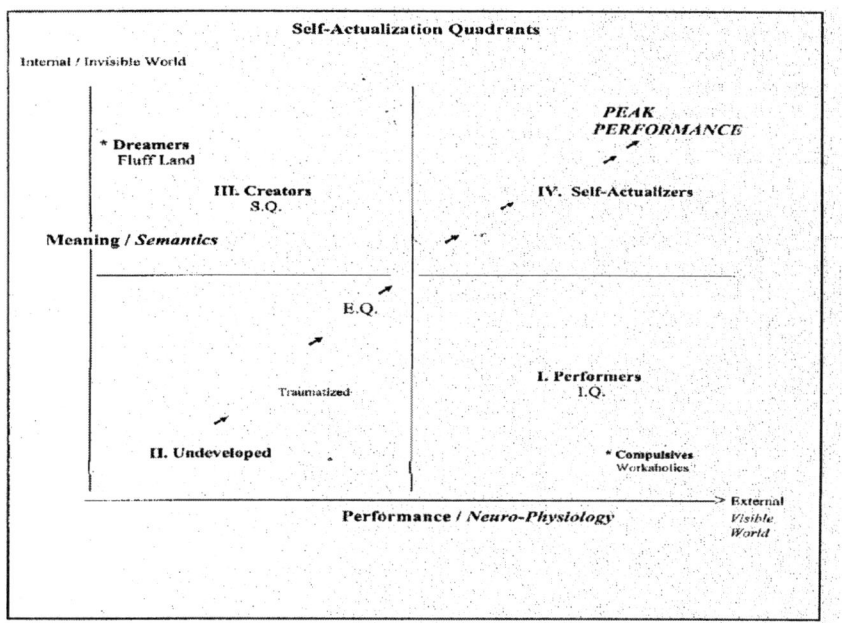

Figure 3. Self-Actualization Quadrant.

The matrix of the self-actualization quadrants facilitate the Meta-Coach in training to move through the meaning/performance matrices or quadrants to move toward peak performance. Maslow referred to self-actualization as moments of peak experiences. The quadrant has two axis's. One axis, the axis of meaning, is the meanings one gives to things, including performances. The second

138

is the axis of performance, the ability to perform. This is similar to the flow diagram that Csikszentmihalyi developed.[121] The more meaning one gives toward ones' performance, the greater the peak experience. Thus if a person is a performer, but does not give much meaning to the performance, that person may be considered obsessive compulsive. If the person has neither performance nor meaning, that person is considered underdeveloped.

There are then the dreamers, those who have high meaning, but little transfer into performance of that meaning. And finally there are those who through coaching and state-management are able to have high meaning and excellent performance, and thus are able to have peak experiences. Hall states that the Self-Actualization Quadrants is "a model based on the actualizing of potentials being a function of meaning and performance, based on 12 meta-programs." [122] The quadrants can be used by the Meta-Coach trainee's to determine how their meaning and performance align.

---

[121] Csikszentmihali, M. (1975). *Beyond boredom and anxiety*. San Francisco: Jossey-Bass
[122] Hall (2006) p. 14

On the third day another axis from the Axis of Change model is described. This is the axis of decision to change. Once it is determined that there is enough away from and toward energy, and the client is ready to make a decision, the client may be reflective or may be ready to act. The Meta-Coach trainee learns to listen to the client to determine where they are on this axis. The Meta-Coach trainee can either probe the client if the client's state is one of reflecting on the decision, and they are not ready to move toward action; if this is the case then the Meta-Coach will probe into the client's matrix in order to understand his or her reflections. If the client is ready to make the decision for change and has moved past reflection, the Meta-Coach trainee learns how to be the provoker, to provoke the client toward action. Along with this second axis of change, the Meta-Coach trainee is learning about the other matrices of the mind that affect how the client, and even the Meta-Coach trainee, how they themselves process and believe thoughts about meaning and about self. As has already been stated in this literature review, the Matrix of the mind includes the matrix of meaning, how a person gives meaning, and a matrix about what they think of themselves, or the self matrix.

The Meta-Coach trainee learns about how they construct meaning and what they give meaning to as well as they learn about what they believe, value, find interesting etc. about themselves. There are several methods that the Meta-Coach trainee's learn and experience about how to understand their own Matrix. One of those methods is a step back skill. It is the skill to reflect on ones' feelings, belief's, frames, etc. Another method the Meta-Coach trainee learns is to use meta-questions to elicit and explore meaning and self, as well as the other matrices of the mind of power, time, others, and the world. There are 26 meta-questions the Meta-Coach trainee learns that gives them access into his or her own matrices of his or her mind and of the clients. These questions explore meaning and elicit states. The meta-questions are not to create states or direct states, but to elicit the clients own states and to increase the level of those states. The meta-questions are not to change a client, but to allow the client the opportunity to experience the matrix of his or her mind.

Another learning and experience that the Meta-Coach trainee gets from the training of day three is coming to an understanding of cognitive distortions and how to update his or her cognitive

141

distortions. Cognitive distortions are one's styles or the mode of thinking. They are the patterns in which one filters information, usually unconscious patterns that can be brought to light and updated so as to increase self-actualization. According to Hall and Duval cognitive distortions are identified as part of Rational-Emotive Behavioral Therapy. These distortions in how a person cognates or thinks affect how one filters and views the world and thus has an effect on the self-actualization of the Meta-Coach trainee and the client. There are 13 cognitive distortions as listed by Hall and Duval and cognitive counters to reduce or eliminate the destructive distortions that could hinder the growth of an individual. The follow lists the distortion and the counters to that distortion. These are ways that a person thinks and ways of improving the distortions of that thinking.

1. Over-Generalizing – Being too general so that one jumps to conclusions without using all the facts. If the Meta-Coach in training recognizes this cognitive distortion in him or herself or a client, they may counter the over-generalization by developing a frame of contextual thinking. This is the opposite over-generalization and is

about asking questions about what, when, where, how, who, etc.

2. All-or-Nothing Thinking – This is either-or-thinking or what others have called 'thinking only in black and white.' If one has this cognitive distortion the person would think something is or is not, there is no middle ground. If the Meta-Coach trainee recognizes this cognitive distortion in self or client, they may counter the all-or-nothing thinking by using both-and-thinking. It is to intentionally consider if this is the only way to recognize something. Is it possible that other options, other than all-or-nothing are possible?

3. Labeling – This is labeling or name calling. Over-generalizing so that something becomes static and is given a label as if it is equal to that label. If the Meta-Coach trainee recognizes this cognitive distortion in them self, he or she may counter the labeling by being led to test reality. Does this experience or thing demand that it is labeled? Is it the label? Is this thing that was labeled really the noun that it has been given, or is it a verb?

4. Blaming – This is when one does not take the blame for anything. It is always someone else's fault, someone else is

responsible, and not the person. If the Meta-Coach trainee recognizes this cognitive distortion in them self, he or she may counter blaming by doing a reality test. What really caused the event that was blamed on others? Use information to determine all the factors involved.

5. Mind-Reading – This is when one projects thoughts, frames, and maps onto the person who he or she is communicating with. If the Meta-Coach trainee recognizes this cognitive distortion in them self or client, they may counter mind-reading by focusing on what is really going on. What behaviors are seen? What does the other person mean by what he or she says?

6. Prophesying – This is when a person takes a negative attitude and projects it into the future, as if the present will always be and the future is the consequent of an antecedent current. If the Meta-Coach trainee recognizes this cognitive distortion in them self they may counter prophesying by gathering information about what really causes things to happen? What forces are really at play? Keeping open the options that life is a process and that he

or she can become responsible for the own future and help direct it, no matter what has or is happening.

7. Emotionalizing – Believing that one's emotions are reality, and not the difference between the map and the territory. If the Meta-Coach trainee recognizes this cognitive distortion in them self or client, he or she may counter emotionalizing by thinking critically about the cause of the emotions. How is the map and the experience different?

8. Personalizing – Perceiving the actions of others as being about them self. Taking things as personal and about them, when in reality it was not about them. If the Meta-Coach trainee recognizes this cognitive distortion in them self, he or she may counter personalizing by doing a reality test to see if the content and context are really about them. One way to do that is to take a third person perspective on it.

9. Awfulizing – "This is awful!" Taking the worst possible scenario perspective on things. If the Meta-Coach trainee recognizes this cognitive distortion in them self, he or she may counter awfulizing by reviewing how he or she labels things. He or she needs to do a reality check to understand

cause and effect and how the frames and meaning affect this frame.

10. Should-ing – These are the rules, you must do this, and you should do this. If the Meta-Coach trainee recognizes this cognitive distortion in them self or the client, he or she may counter should-ing by asking what is that rule? Where did it come from? Says who? He or she may change from "should", to, "I would prefer that."

11. Filtering – This is having tunnel vision. It is filtering out things and only looking or accepting ideas from one perspective. If the Meta-Coach trainee cognizes this recognizes distortion in them self, he or she may counter filtering by focusing on all the content, looking for different perspectives and both sides, looking from a third person perspective.

12. Can't-ing – This is using the word 'can't.' Imposing limits on self and others by stating it can't be done. If the Meta-Coach trainee recognizes this cognitive distortion in them self, he or she may counter can't-ing by using possibility thinking. Asking, "What stop's you? What if you did?"

13. Discounting – This is to put down possible solutions to problems. It is discounting possibilities as possibilities. If the Meta-Coach trainee recognizes this cognitive distortion in them self, he or she may counter discounting by using appreciative thinking. It is working to recognize value and asking, what does count?

Also during day three of the Meta-Coach Training the Meta-Coach trainee learns and experiences the matrix of self. He or she come to understand the frames of self and how those frames affect them self and identify them self as a Meta-Coach. Part of the self-matrix development for the Meta-Coach trainee and for what he or she learns to bring to the client, is creating acceptance, appreciation, and creating ago-strength.

Key Relevant Topics of Day 4:
Day four consists of some activities that are focused on the development of the individuals personal or business plan. The Meta-Coach trainee learns about the Benchmarking model and the business and life plan. And, even though these activities are part of Meta-Coach training, the content or processes are not delineated in

this chapter. The actual process and learning develops the Meta-Coach further, and thus positively influences the Meta-Coach trainee and the ability to coach a client toward self-actualization.

A key event outside of the benchmarking and life/business plan is another matrix, the matrix of power. This matrix is how one understands power – the power to possess and do, and the lack of power to posses and do. There are a few patterns that the Meta-Coach trainee goes through to recognize the matrix and to use the matrix of power to increase his or her self-actualization. Hall and Duval state, "The Power Matrix is the second most important one after the Self matrix." [123] This power meaning affects everything because it affects the idea that one has about his or her intentionality. Though one may have intention to do, that person may have a weak frame of power and not believe that he or she can intentionally do what he or she wants to do.

A pattern that the Meta-Coach trainee learns during day four is called the de-contamination pattern. The Meta-Coach trainee

---

[123] Hall L. M., & Duval, M. (2006). *The international meta-coaching training system.* Clifton, CO: Neuro-Semantic Publications p. 132

learns and experiences how to get the ego out of the way so he or she can work with a client. The first thing the Meta-Coach trainee has to do is identify the facets of them self that will have an effect on the ego and how that can negatively affect the coaching relationship. The second thing the Meta-Coach trainee has to do is identify what needs to be removed so the ego does not get in the way. Then the Meta-Coach trainee needs to recognize what he or she needs on the heart and mind. Then the trainee decontaminates by going through a process, and finally, this has to all be coached to the body so the body experiences what the mind thinks and feels and the trainee has a single mind-body-emotion.

Another thing or pattern that the Meta-Coach trainee does on day four is setting responsibility to/for frames. This pattern is to have the Meta-Coach trainee understand that he or she is responsible for them self. The Meta-Coach has to take responsibility for the rapport and coaching environment with the client. The Meta-Coach trainee learn that he or she are not responsible for the client and how the client feels or thinks, but only how he or she feels and thinks. This is a pattern where the Meta-Coach trainee accesses a previous created power zone where he or she are in a state to recognize and own the power to emote, to think, speak, and to behave. The Meta-Coach trainee develops a state and understanding that he or she owns those powers – nobody else does. No one gives those powers and nobody can take them away. When the emotions or thinking or speaking or behaving happens, even in response to others, it was still within the power of the Meta-Coach and not anyone else. A full experience of this state and power zone would eliminate from the vocabulary the expression "he made me do that", "she made me mad", "they made me say that." Owning your power zone, the Meta-Coach can own his or her powers to emote, think, speak, and behave.

Thus there is also in day four of the Meta-Coaching training patterns and experiences for the Meta-Coach trainee that adds further to his or her ability to increase the measure of self-actualization. The Meta-Coach trainees are learning patterns and models for giving this capability to their clients as well. So, from day one of the Meta-Coaching Training, until day four of the Meta-Coaching Training, there is a progressive growth in the opportunity for the Meta-Coach to reach higher levels of self-actualization.

Key Relevant Topics of Day 5:

During day five of the Meta-Coach Training, there are again learning and experiences that the Meta-Coaching trainee goes through that increase his or her potential toward self-actualization. It is on this day that the other Axis of Change areas of Co-Creating/Testing and Actualizing Inner and Outer Games and the Matrix of 'other' that is explored.

The third axis of change is when the client is ready for change and either he or she has an inner game going on or are ready for action and have an external reference, he or she has an outer game. The Meta-Coach trainee learns to recognize where the client is in the axis and if the client has the energy for change and has made the decision to change, the Meta-Coach may either work with the inner, if that is where the client is, and co-create the activity internally. If the client is ready to actualize the well formed outcome that has been the focus of the coaching client relationship, the Meta-Coach will help facilitate the client in actualizing that potential.

As the Meta-Coach trainee learns about this axis, they go from the will to do, the decision to finally do, and are now there – he or she is in the doing phase. If the Meta-Coach trainee goes through the same process as he or she experiences the training environment, then by the time the Meta-Coach trainee is at that stage of developing states, frames, and games, he or she has further ability to self-actualize.

The matrix of the frame of 'other', that is, how one views others is another area that is reviewed and experienced on day five. The Meta-Coach trainee develops an understanding of his or her matrix of how he or she views others and the Meta-Coach trainee learns how to walk the client through the same process.

Key Relevant Topics of Day 6:
On day six the key relevant topics that greatly affect the self-actualizing potential of the Meta-Coach trainee is the final matrix of his or her view and belief of the world and the final Axis of Change of solidification, that is, integrating, reinforcing, and testing the new change. The key learning and experiences of the world matrix is the usage of developing the rest of the coaching business plans.

152

One's matrix of the world affects how one plans to act, be, and do in the world. They Meta-Coach trainee has thus far worked with other Meta-Coach trainees to coach the business plan. In the new frames of the Meta-Coach, engendered by all this work toward his or her coaching business, there is a new energy toward actualizing all that he or she learned and experienced and there is a deeper level of actualization taking place.

The final axis on the Axis of Change Model is solidifying the new change by the client and testing to ensure that the change is real and if there are more changes to come. It is the final axis on the Axis of Change Model. This final step can be the start of another change because the change model is not a linear model, but a systemic model and dance with the client through the complete change process. The model gives the coach areas in which to understand where the client may be in the process and some tools or methods to facilitate and mobilize the client to the change he or she desires. This final axis would be the place where the client is encouraged for a job well done as well as a place to ensure the change stays in place.

Key Relevant Topics of Day 7:

On day seven, the final matrix of the seven matrices is the time matrix. The time matrix asks, where do we live our lives? Do we live predominantly in the past, present, or future? What type of a relationship does one have with time? Is time a friend or an enemy? Is the person's life governed by things not yet to come? Is the person's life governed by what has happened in the past?

Key Relevant Topics of Day 8:

Day eight wraps things up and the Self-Actualization Quadrants and the Matrix as a system are discussed. The Self-Actualization Quadrants are already discussed in this literature review and the Matrix has already been described. The Matrix is covered as a system, rather than a linear model on this eighth day. This eighth day is a reinforcement of the Matrix model as it is defined as systemic, and thus reinforces what has already been observed and written about as his or her relationship to the self-actualizing of the trainee.

Conclusion of Chapter Six

The Meta-Coach trainee then, upon being benchmarked on seven key skills of listening, support, questioning, meta-questioning, state-inducing, receiving feedback, and giving feedback graduates and is certified as an Associate Meta-Coach.

It is now time to get into some of the pragmatics of this kaizen philosophy. An overview of Kaizen, of Self-Actualization, motivation, return on investment, transfer of training, and of the Meta-Coach training has taken place. It is now time to bring this all together and review how the models of the Meta-Coach could be integrated into a Coaching Conversation around the sustained Kaizen culture.

Chapter Seven

The NLP Communication Model and Continuous Improvement

There are seven models that the Meta-Coach learns and uses in his or her coaching conversation with the client. The Meta-Coach is armed with models that structure the dance with the client. These models, segregated and integrated within the coaching conversation bring about self-actualizing changes in the client and therefore bring about the cultural shift from knowing about Kaizen to doing Kaizen. What would you rather have, knowledge but no doing? Or knowledge and doing? The Meta-Coach, through the use of these seven models, facilitates the integration of knowledge and action to bring about a Kaizen culture.

One of the models that the Meta-Coach uses in the coaching conversation is the NLP communication model. NLP stands for 'Neuro-Linguistic Programming' and is a model of how the human being experiences and communicates that experience both to themselves as well as to each other.

A key component of NLP is that each of us experiences the world through how we represent that world in the theater of our minds. When we experience external stimulus through our eyes, our ears, our body, our tastes, and olfactory (smells) we then store that experience in the system that we experienced it with. If a person see's an event, and hears something with that event, he or she will store, in his or her neurology that event as a bio-chemical process. Brain neurons will create electrical-chemical links through the synapses and those links will re-fire when that original stimulus is remembered.

Some people will naturally use their eyes more than their ears to experience the world. Others will use their ears more than their eyes. Other people will use their body, their kinesthetic to experience the world. They are the people that use words such as 'I feel you' instead of 'I hear where you are coming from' or 'I see where you are coming from.' These different systems are called the VAK systems. VAK stands for Visual, Auditory, and Kinesthetic.

When a people start to think, they think with their mind-body-emotions. Those thinking patterns will be represented by either

157

pictures in the mind, sounds in the head, language spoken in the head, feelings in the body, and sometimes smells or tastes. Close your eyes and re-experience a great experience you had. Do you see pictures? Do you hear sounds or voices? Do you smell anything or taste anything? We all represent the world in the theater of our minds.

The NLP model works with these representational systems and through the process of editing those movies, it changes the experience. The NLP model teaches the person that they are the director, the editor, and the producer of their movies. So, change the movies, and you change the experience.

Another aspect of playing movies in our heads is that those movies affect how we receive new incoming stimulus. If a person is a visual person he or she may only learn when he or she sees, but not learn when he or she hears. If a person is kinesthetic, he or she may only learn when he or she can do and not learn if he or she only listens. The VAK system and understanding each person's VAK system affects how they can be managed, trained, and lead.

158

Our VAK systems act as natural unconscious filters in how we experience the world. When there is an interaction between two people in an organization and that interaction is to build a Kaizen culture, that interaction is only as strong as the VAK systems match. If the trainer, mentor, or coach works from their own VAK system and if it is different than the VAK system of the other person, much gets lost in the translation and the training, mentoring, or coaching is less effective.

Can you build a Kaizen culture if there is always something blocking the free flow of information? The Meta-Coach learns how to recognize the VAK system of the person he or she coaches and then coach to that VAK system. This change from coaching from the coaches VAK system to coaching to the VAK system of the individual enhances the value of the Kaizen proposition.

Pragmatic Example

Kaizen training can be quite extensive and intense. It includes the ideas of both a process to be followed, a map to be used, content to be learned, and new technical skills to be acquired. When a trainer has a kinesthetic style, and the trainee has an auditory style and leadership has a visual style, what can happen? There can be a miscommunication of the key success factors of the training and implementation.

The trainer is talking in terms of the *physical* necessities and how they _feel_ that it's important to do a thorough measurement systems analysis. But the trainee pays attention to the former statement about *hearing* what the customer wants and that we have to *listen* to their requirements of measurement. The Supervisor gets on the floor to track the project and *looks* at the sample to *see* that at least the trainee has them for the project. Each of these three people may be on a different page because of how they represent the world. And all along the trainer was so sure he was clear, and can simply scratch his head as to why the trainee and supervisor where ok with just making sure that they *heard* the customer's requirements and *saw* this process take place instead of *physically* measuring the data for a good measurement system analysis.

The start of the developing of this Kaizen culture then depends on the communication between the trainer, the trainee, and leadership. Because of how people filter information and how that subsequently affects the communication of each of these people or groups, it is imperative that the NLP communication model guide this communication. The Meta-Coach is trained and fluid in coaching each of these groups through their representational systems, thereby, bringing clear communication which facilitates clear conversations that enhance this transfer and thus adds assurance to the development of this necessary cultural change that encourages the opportunity of a competitive advantage.

Chapter Eight

The Meta-States Model of Reflexivity and Continuous

Improvement

What is a Meta-State? What is Meta? What is State? Meta means to go above something. State means the current mood or frame of mind. We never leave home without a state. When we go to sleep, we are in a state. When we wake up, we are in a state. A Meta-State is a state about a state. If a person sees a defect in a product they have a first level representation of that defect. They simply notice the defect. As they think about that defect they may go into a state of curiousness, how did that defect take place? They now went Meta to the first state of simply seeing the defect, now they are curious about what they saw. Then the person may be angry that they are curious because they are a Six Sigma Black Belt and they should know what caused that defect. This is a Meta-Meta State. They are angry at their curiosity of their impression. Then they may feel stupid because they feel angry at their curiosity of their impression. This is a Meta-Meta-Meta State; and this can go up and up.

162

A state, a mood, an attitude, these are all one and the same. How does a state come about? There are multiple levels of reality and thought that intertwine in a process that ultimately develop a state. Also, states are not permanent fixtures that do not change but can change moment by moment. Now glad, now mad, now excited, now calm; process to process. How are these states brought to birth?

Take a look around you. What do you see? If you are outside you may see the sky, some trees, some buildings, roads, cars. If you are inside you may see a desk, a chair, a wall, a picture, a light, another person. These are all things that are outside, they exist in the world. They, these things, these nouns, can never enter into you. They feel like they do, you see the tree, the cloud, the wall, the person. But, they are now and always outside your world.

In the next level you have you senses, you can see, you can feel, you can smell, you can taste, you can hear. But those are organs of senses. They are part of your person and they sense, they pick up external stimulus from the world. They do not convey information to you. They do not give you names, information, senses, etc. they only *pick up* stimulus from that world that is outside of you.

The next level is your neural network. These are all the neurons, probably about 100 billion of them. These neurons are all interconnected with synapses. They barely touch each other. There is a small microscopic gap between the branches of synapses between the billions and billions of cells. This gap is called the synaptic gap. Between these gaps, chemicals, neuro-transmitters and neuro-modulators flow. When these flow, they cause electrical stimulus to run the length of that neuron to the other neurons that it is connected too. In a split second, your sense organs (eyes, ears, mouth, nose, body) pick up information from this outside world and it gets processed through these neural networks.

The next level is that these neural networks, in a split second build a map of that world. It is like a fax machine. It takes a picture of those sights, sounds, tastes, feelings, and smells and represents them in your head. It is at this level that you start to make sense of the world that is out there. Now, the world that is out there is offering your senses trillions of bits of information, but your senses can only take in a very small fraction of that world, how does it know what to take in, and what to leave out?

The next level of interaction between you and the external world is your idea, your feelings, your beliefs, your likes, you dislikes etc, of all that is now represented to you from this world. Those ideas, feelings, beliefs, likes, dislikes etc. are what determine what out of the trillions of bits of information will be allowed into your mind-body-emotions. You are now in a state. That state is the result of all these levels of activity and interaction between you and the outside world.

At the next level and levels beyond that is where you then feel about your feeling, you value, your believing, you dislike, your idea, etc. This is your Meta-State. You now have a state about a state. And, let me add, in the mix of all this is your meanings and your intentions. The meanings you hold in mind are mixed with your willful intentions, and then filtered from a trillion down to a few billion, make up your state. Your feelings, beliefs, values, interests, etc., about those billion filtered stimuli make up your Meta-States.

Knowing all this, that each of us, your executive, middle manager, and employee, lives in this process of the transfer of external stimulus to internal representations and then ultimate feelings and beliefs about those representations and then feelings and beliefs about those feelings and beliefs, should challenge us to find ways to manage these states for optimum performance; Kaizen!

As a person starts to reflect on themselves and how they feel (kinesthetic) about Kaizen they may feel excited about it. Being excited about Kaizen may be the corporate vision and the person may then think of Kaizen as important to their career. This importance to their career then adds flavor to Kaizen and Kaizen may take on a whole new meaning. As we can see, Kaizen has a meaning as was discussed at the beginning of this book, but now we see that Kaizen can take on other meanings. To the employee, does Kaizen mean job security? What if a person has to use Kaizen and he or she cannot understand the content of Kaizen events and he or she then associates Kaizen with lack of understanding, then with fear of lack of understanding because if he or she does not understand Kaizen events, he or she may lose his or her jobs or his or her status in the company. At that point, Kaizen no longer means constant improvement, but a threat to ones safety. How will a person perform if Kaizen means threat and not constant improvement?

We are the meaning makers. Any idea that we hold in our minds is a meaning. When your executive thinks of Kaizen, does it mean the same thing to them as it does to your middle management? Does it mean the same thing to your worker on the shop floor? If meaning exists in the individual (where else does it exist?) then how do you develop a culture of Kaizen if everyone has a different meaning and how do you build common meaning if you do not first develop a way to communicate across the different VAK systems?

There are many things that should be taken into consideration as a person thinks about developing a Kaizen culture. There is training, there is missions, there are visions, there are strategies, there are transfer of training models, there is mentoring. Yet, each and every one of these ways to facilitate the Kaizen culture is dependent on the state of those who will be using Kaizen in their everyday jobs. It is this most critical function of culture that is usually the least thought about or even never thought about.

If your executive, your middle manager, and your employees come to work in a state, is that state conducive to Kaizen? Does the state support Kaizen? Does the state reflect Kaizen? Is the state antagonistic to Kaizen? When the worker needs to be trained, are they in a learning state? When the middle managers need to plan for a Kaizen event, is the middle manager in the correct state? When your executive is designing a long term strategy for Kaizen implementation and for Kaizen culture, is he or she in a state of Kaizen? The state determines the behavior, the behavior determines the results. The Meta-Coach process facilitates the executive, the middle manager, and the employee in state management; this enables the organization to manage their states, states that are conducive to the Kaizen goal.

Once the states can be managed and everyone gives the same meaning to Kaizen and that meaning supports the corporate goals and strategy, you are on your way to a culture of Kaizen. Once this meaning starts to affect the movement (motivation) of the leader, worker, and trainer, then it is time to plan and implement and control for Kaizen. To do this, and maintain this momentum, what process or model will be followed to ensure that the culture is enriched and the competitive advantage is assured?

Chapter Nine

The Axis of Change Model and Continuous Improvement

The Axis of Change Model was introduced in the chapter on motivation. This chapter will go into deeper detail on the Axis of Change and on how the Axis of Change reflects a natural process of change from a non or average Kaizen culture to a Kaizen, Kaizen culture.

The Axis of Change model is a model of change. It is the process in which change naturally takes place. The Meta-Coach uses this model to follow and to lead the dance with the client through the coaching conversation to bring about a Kaizen culture.

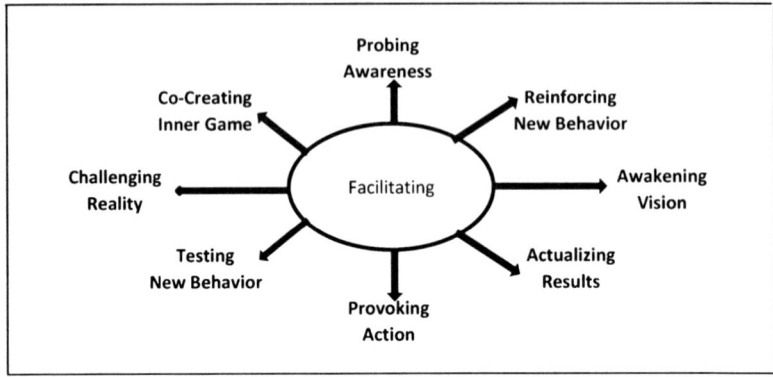

The Axis of Change Model uses the four mechanisms of change for self-actualization. The first axis is the axis of motivation. One of the tools or methods of Kaizen is Design for Six Sigma. The process of Design for Six Sigma will be used as we walk through this change model.

The Axis of Motivation

Usually the first step in developing a Design for Six Sigma process is to train engineers in the Design for Six Sigma method. Normally engineers are trained in Design for Six Sigma and then they find ways to use what they have been trained to use. But, the challenge is retaining all that is taught and then using that which is retained back in the work place. The Axis of Change of motivation has two ends. There is a moving away from something and then there is moving toward something.

This axis elicits thoughts and feelings and beliefs about new possibilities. About a brighter future, about new potentials and these beliefs and feelings move the person toward a goal. This axis also includes the moving away from something. This end of the axis discovers and faces with reality the discomfort of staying where one is at. In every choice of movement, there is a movement from something and a movement toward something. The motivation part of the Axis of Change is a propulsion system. It is an energy system, pushing away from pain and discomfort and pulling toward pleasure and comfort.

The engineer, to be challenged to use the newly learned material would be coached from the 'away from' axis.' On this axis the engineer is challenged to move away from something. Have they had enough of bad launches? Bad products? Lost profits? Poor performance? The other end of the axis is the 'awakener.' It is moving the engineer toward something. Toward defect free products. Toward less time spent at the customer? Toward finally meeting timing or benchmarks.

It is only after the engineer has sufficient propulsion, away and from, that the engineer is ready to move toward the decision to use what they have learned. These examples apply to any type of change that a person wants to make. This Axis of Change is a tool for the Meta-Coach to facilitate the motivation of the execututive, middle manager, or first line employee to move out into the Kaizen experience.

The Axis of Decision

Once an engineer feels the propulsion to move out and away from not doing Design for Six Sigma the next natural step in the change process is to start to make the change. It is the Decision of Change Axis. Some people spend more time reflecting on the choice to make change than others. Some people, after they have the motivation to make change, just go for it. Others need to reflect and plan before they commit to making the change. The Meta-Coach asks probing questions of the engineer to drive the engineer into self-reflexivity until they can make the decision to make a decision to use Design for Six Sigma. The Axis of Decision applies to any natural change process and includes your executive or middle manager who desires to develop a Kaizen culture.

Once the engineer, through reflection to the probing questions of the Meta-Coach may make the decision to make a decision. The Meta-Coach then changes the questioning style to that of a provoker. The Engineer is provoked into making a decision that they have thoroughly reflected on because they felt the propulsion of motivation driving them.

The Axis of Creation

Once the engineer has decided to use Design for Six Sigma they need to determine how they will do it? When will they do it? With whom will they do it? And remember, in the mix of all this, the engineer is carrying around his or her VAK system and all the layers of meaning that he or she has about Kaizen and Design for Six Sigma.

The Axis of Creation is also known as the inner game and the outer game. All of us play an inner and outer game. The inner game is when the engineer is creating the plan for the use of Design for Six Sigma. It is a thinking game. It is a co-creating with the Coach. The Engineer is reflecting and planning on how he or she will use his or her new learned skills.

Once the Meta-Coach and the engineer have a plan of creation in place, the next step is in actualizing what the inner game created. This is when the engineer moves from the inner game of creating the plan to the outer game of performing Design for Six Sigma. The inner and outer game of creation is the natural way that people change and applies to the change of culture desired by the executive or the change in product development by the middle manager.

The Axis of Solidification

The final axis on the Axis of Change is the Axis of Solidification. This is the final step in the change process. When a person makes a change and has gone through all the other steps there is a testing of the decision. Was it the right decision? Does it fit with other decisions? This is again where we see the important role of the meanings that the engineer has about Kaizen or about Design for

Six Sigma. This is where the Meta-Coach asks supporting questions of the engineer. This is where the Meta-Coach reinforces the decision of the engineer.

The final step on the axis of solidification is that of testing the change. The Meta-Coach facilitates the engineer in analyzing the decision, the action. This is where the change is tested. What else do you need to do? What else will you do now that you took this action? This is the final phase that people naturally go through when they make a sustainable change. The person will oftentimes dance through the Axis of Change as they change in motivation, change in decision, change in creation, but the Meta-Coach facilitates this change and through the process of working in the engineers VAK system and within their unique meaning making, the change toward a Kaizen culture solidifies.

This whole process of meta-states, NLP, axis of change, transfer of training, etc. takes communication and commitment to language and interactions. This is a challenge to all those involved from the worker, the leader, the trainer, and the coach. What methods or models direct this challenge? As the coach uses this model, how does the behavior of the coach transfer to the behavior of the leader or worker, what coaching behaviors do they learn from this process from the coach? And, what skills does the coach learn and is benchmarked on that ensures that he or she can actually perform this type of necessary cultural change?

Chapter Ten

The Benchmarking Model and Kaizen

Another model that the Meta-Coach uses as they coach your executive, middle manager and employee is the Benchmarking model. The Benchmarking model is an expanded Meta-Model, which is a model of communication. The Benchmarking model is a model that operationalizes the intangible and the soft skills of listening, rapport, support, questioning, etc.

The Meta-Coach is evaluated on using the skills of listening, the skill of supporting, the skill of asking questions and meta-questions, the skill of giving and receiving feedback.

Benchmarking Listening

The first Benchmark measures the Meta-Coach's ability to listen, to be present with the leader. Does the Meta-Coach interrupt the leader? Is the Meta-Coach doing all the talking? Does the Meta-Coach only do part of the talking? Does the Meta-Coach paraphrase the leader or do they feed back the exact words of the leader and thus entering into the leader's world and not push their own world view.

When the Meta-Coach has skills of mastery when it comes to listening they will be speaking less than 20% of the time, giving the leader the time to speak. They will ask about what is not being said and invite the leader to ask themselves questions they have never asked before.

Benchmarking Supporting

The next skill that the Meta-Coach learns and becomes proficient with is that of supporting the leader. The Meta-Coach offers support by creating an environment where they make the leader feel welcome so they can share his or her thoughts, emotions, fears, needs, etc. Supporting includes building rapport with the leader. It is matching the leader's world, the leaders's semantic space, the leader's posture. The leader operates from his or her world view and from his or her matrix of the world. The Meta-Coach learns how to build solid rapport with the leader so that the communication between the two is like a beautiful dance; and dance that facilitates the needed change to bring about Kaizen.

Benchmarking Questions and Meta-Questions

The next two skills that are part of the Benchmarking model are that of questioning and meta-questioning. The Meta-Coach facilitates the leader through a process where the leader uses his or her resources in new profound ways. The Meta-Coach does this facilitation by asking the right questions at the right times. The questions are guided by the world view of the leader and by where that leader is in relation to the Axis of Change.

Leaders are also asked questions about the responses that they offered, making those questions meta-questions. If an engineer is asked "what stops you from using Design for Six Sigma" and they answer, "my boss just does not give me the time to use it;" the Meta-Coach may ask "and what do you believe about not having enough time to use it?" That is a Meta-Question. The Meta-Coach asks questions and Meta-Questions to facilitate the mobilization of the client's resources.

Benchmarking Inducing States

Another skill that is part of the Benchmarking model is that of inducing states. We are always in state. As you read this you may be in a state of interest, a state of excitement, a state of learning, or even a board state. We never leave home without our state and our state changes as the hours change. The Meta-Coach is skilled in inducing the right states at the right time to facilitate the change that the leader wants; the state of joy because you used Kaizen principles on the last project.

Benchmarking Giving and Receiving Feedback

The other two skills that are part of the Benchmarking model are skills in giving feedback to the leader, and skills in receiving feedback. The Meta-Coach is skilled and benchmarked against a set of questions and meta-questions that drive to the heart of the Meta-Coach giving feedback and being able to receive feedback.

The Meta-Coaching time with the leader is a time of fierce conversation where your executive, middle manager, and employee (each separately of course) have a serious, probably the most serious, personal, upfront conversation of their lives, and within this conversation there is always feedback to the leader and the leader will have feedback comments to the Meta-Coach. The Meta-Coach must be able to give and receive feedback.

181

The feedback that the Meta-Coach is benchmarked on is not just being able to receive feedback or give feedback, but to denominalize (verbs that were turned into nouns) their feedback. Benchmarks are about what one can see, feel, smell, task, and hear. The Meta-Coach learns to *'see'* and *'hear'* and not just feel, feedback to the leader must be sensory based. "I noticed that every time you mention Six Sigma you roll your eyes to the left, what are you experiencing when you do that?"

Given that the coach has been benchmarked and certified that they can walk the leader through these steps toward affecting them to create this Kaizen culture, what other areas do they work with? Does not each leader or worker have a sense of who they are? Or a sense of the power they have at work? What about the leader and his or her perception of how hard others will work on Kaizen?

Chapter Eleven

The Matrix Model and Kaizen

The Matrix of Self

What is the matrix? The matrix is the womb where you live. Inside your matrix you carry with you your meaning of self. In the matrix you have your self-identity. Your self acceptance, your self love, your self esteem. Everywhere you go you do not leave home without it. When people talk to you or offend you, your ego kicks in and your ego is your construct, it is of your making. Throughout your life your parents, your siblings, your teachers, your leaders, your friends, your relatives, etc. all helped you frame your construct of self. If you were loved and cherished, if your parents told you that you were worth the entire world to them, you probably developed a concept of self that is worthy and cherished.

If your family or friends constantly told you that you were good for nothing, then you may have a self identity as someone who does not amount to much. So what point am I trying to make? The point is, is that your concept of self is YOUR concept. It is a concept that you started learning before your first birthday and that learning

183

helped set your frames of how you have seen yourself ever since. Your concept of you and the concept of self that your senior executive has of themselves, the identity that your middle manager has of themselves, and the identity your person on the shop floor has of themselves drastically affects how they relate to Kaizen events.

To some executives, middle managers, and employees learning the tools of Kaizen like Six Sigma or Design for Six Sigma may affect their personal beliefs about themselves. What personal beliefs do your executives, middle managers, or floor employees have about themselves? How do you know? How does their view of their self affect their performance as leaders of Kaizen?

The Matrix of Power
Another content of our matrix that we never leave home without is our Matrix of Power. The Matrix of Power is the beliefs that a person has about his or her skills and abilities. These skills may include the learning of the skill, the doing of the skill, and even the power that is gained or lost by the learning of the skill.

Every person starts to develop his or her values and beliefs about his or her personal power very early in life. As a person grows into adult hood he or she brings that sense of power with them and use it to build deeper and wider frames about his or her personal power.

When it comes to Kaizen and a person's power matrix, it becomes very important that your executive, middle manager, or employee at the worker level have a specific belief about their powers. Do they have the power to learn? The power to change? The power to integrate? The power to communicate this new Kaizen culture? Everywhere your executive goes, his or hers Matrix of Power is sure to follow, in fact, they live within that Matrix.

The Matrix of Others

Culture is the shared norms, beliefs, and values of a group of people. To develop a Kaizen culture there needs to be shared norms, beliefs, and values around the Kaizen event or Kaizen philosophy. Your executive, middle manager, and employee has learned how and what to believe about other people. Are other people friendly? Do other people support you in your endeavors?

Will others be truthful and honest, or will the tell lies to get their own ways?

What your executive believes about others has a dramatic affect on how well they develop and maintain a culture of Kaizen. If they hold to a theory 'x' that people are generally lazy that will have an effect on how they perceive the transfer of training and the use of Kaizen. If your middle manager holds negative beliefs about trainers or about executives who demand change (like a new Kaizen culture) it will have a devastating effect on his or her Kaizen performance.

It suddenly becomes quite clear that everyone, from your executive down to your working employee, each person carries within the matrix of their mind a whole host of people. Their past bosses, wives, husbands, friends, enemies, relatives, teachers, employees, etc. These people can become voices and guides in ones view of how others are. To successfully develop a Kaizen culture it becomes imperative that those involved delve into the Matrix of their minds to understand their beliefs, interests, and values about others.

186

The Matrix of Time

Time is an interesting construct. Some people live as though time does not exist. They spend their days doing what they know needs to be done, but they do not let the clock tell them if they are late or early. Others cannot help but to keep an eye on the watch. They are on time for every meeting and they make sure every meeting ends when it is supposed to.

Everywhere a person goes he or she bring this concept of time with them —he or she lives either in time or through time. In time is where time is only on the clock, but internally, they live according to their own time. Those that are through time live as if the clock were real and their internal clock must align with the clock on the wall.

Another construct of time is the past, the present, and the future. Some or your executives, middle managers, and employees may spend most of their time in the past. They live in the nostalgia. They live in how things were in the good old days; the good old days before all this Kaizen stuff. We used to just do our jobs and we did them right. Then there are some of your executives, middle managers, employees who live in the future. Kaizen is just a phase, we will be doing something more, something different, we cannot spend much time or energy on Kaizen because it is a phase we are going through and we will be doing something new in the future.

There may also be some of your executives, middle managers, and floor employee's who live in the present and are able to reference the past and see into the future as they need to. Kaizen is needed today to bring our company forward. We have had some great things in the past and by doing Kaizen today, we will have a great future.

The Matrix of the World

Everyone brings with them the worlds they have discovered, the worlds they visited. Your executives, middle managers, and employees may have the world of college, the world of hard knocks, the world of offshore utilization, the world of managers or workers etc. The construct of their worlds affects what they think, how they do, and when they do Kaizen.

If your executive lives in the world of academia, and that world has its own opinion on certain Kaizen events, tools, or methods, that will have a impact on their enculturation of Kaizen.

Kaizen itself is a world, the world of Continuous Improvement, the world of competitive advantage. Does your executive, middle manager, and employee have that world as part of their matrix?

Meaning in the Matrix

Self, Power, Others, Time, and World are all content within the matrix of the mind. Everywhere that a person goes he or she carries with them this content and the meanings he or she gives to this content affects how he or she performs. In fact, your executive, middle manager and employee give meaning to everything, not just the five content items in their matrix.

Your executive, middle manager, and floor employee have meanings for Kaizen, for learning, for change, for trying new things, for permanence, for statistics, for being asked to do things, etc. All these meanings affect how well the Kaizen culture is implemented.

The Matrix of Intention

Intention is purpose; purpose both in doing and purpose in being. Your executive, middle manager, and employee all have different intentionality matrixes. Intentionality is that which they give their attention to, so as to intend to reach some desired outcome. Developing an intentional Kaizen culture requires your executive, middle manager, and employee to intend Kaizen and this means that to intend one thing, they must un-intend another. What do your executives, middle managers, and floor employees have to un-intend?

Prior to Kaizen, what were the intentions of your executive? Are the intentions of Kaizen completely new or are they a re-arranged intention? If Kaizen is to be a culture, what will your executive, middle manager, and employee have to intend, and what current intentions will they have to let go of? Can they let go of current intentions?

The State in the Matrix

Your executive comes to work in a state. That state may be left over from his or her home life. What state was he or she in when he or she left home? Happy, sad, mad, glad, inquisitive, scared, etc. Will your executive be able to shift states when he or she gets to work? When he or she does get to work, what states does he or she go into? It depends on the other content matrixes and the intentional and meaning matrix.

If your executives believe theory 'x' (people are lazy), then when they get to work their 'other' matrix will view the floor employee as lazy and this will affect their intention toward them (they may believe they need to push the employee) and then when they approach the employee, it will put them into a state that is not conducive to build a Kaizen culture.

Once we get past the point of all that we have just discussed and the Kaizen culture is developing, how do your executive, middle manager, and your worker perform this new culture, this new Kaizen? How do they get to their best, their best performance?

Chapter Twelve

The Self-Actualization Quadrants and Kaizen

Self-Actualization includes the idea of peak experiences and peak performances. In a Kaizen context, it is critical that your executive, your middle manager, and your employee self-actualize their highest and best in the use of the tools and concepts of Kaizen.

The Self-Actualization Quadrants is a scale of meaning and performance. The Self-Actualizing executive, middle manager, and employee, when moving into peak performance, will have rich meanings to their Kaizen skills, and great skills to their rich meanings.

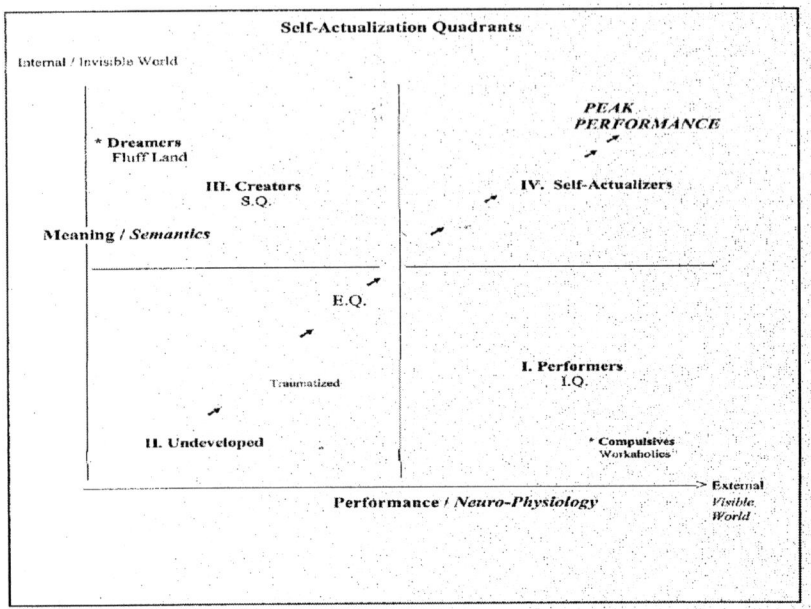

Self-Actualization Quadrants (Hall & Duval, 2006).

If your executive, middle manager, and floor employee have great meanings about Kaizen, but little or no skill, they will spend their time dreaming of Kaizen, but never implementing it. If your executive, your middle manager, and your employee have great skill in Kaizen tools and methods but they give little or no meaning to Kaizen (they do not like Kaizen or think it is useless) then even with all those skills, they will accomplish nothing of lasting value.

193

When your executive, middle manager, and employee have great meanings of Kaizen and what it can do for them and the company, mixed with great skills, they will be part of a team that brings about that Kaizen culture that gives the organization a competitive advantage.

The Meta-Coach, while working through this process of helping you develop your Kaizen culture and thus giving your organization the competitive advantage will also have to follow a plan, a plan of action. Your executive, middle manager, and employee, along with the coach, will need to follow a plan, what plan is the coach familiar with that can meet that need?

Chapter Thirteen

The Matrix Business Plan and Kaizen

Without a plan a person or your organization will never have strategies that focus on the strengths and that eliminate the weaknesses of your organization. There are various types of business plans that your organization can use. There are also various reasons why your organization develops a business plan. The Matrix Business Plan is unique in that it focuses on the Matrix. The five content factors and the process factors in the Matrix: identity, power, others, time, and world, intentionality, state, and meaning.

The Matrix Business plan is not necessarily a high level business plan. It is an action plan that uses a self-reflexive content descriptive plan. There are seven sections to the Matrix Business Plan and each section focuses around a specific content or process of the Matrix Model. As your executive, middle manager, and employee develops their plan for involvement in the Kaizen culture, they reflect, write, and act on a business plan to bring about that sustained culture. They reflect on how their matrix affects their ability to bring about this Kaizen culture.

Now, let's tie it all together!

Chapter Fourteen

Kaizen, Self-Actualization, and the Meta-Coaching Process

This last chapter brings it all together. Kaizen is the continuous improvement of all the processes and procedures that an organization does to change their inputs into outputs that meet or exceed their customers' expectations. Self-actualization is the bringing forth, through the process of growth, the full actuality of that which was only potential. The Meta-Coach Process uses the seven models to develop self-actualization that brings about that sustained Kaizen culture.

The Meta-Coach is trained in the seven models and is trained, from theory to application, how to coach your executive, middle manager, and employee to self-actualize. In the context of Kaizen, the Meta-Coach facilitates the mobilization of the inner and outer resources of your executive, your middle manager, and your employee, to bring about transformational change in what Kaizen means, and in what the skill and tools mean, and what the merging of the two mean.

197

To an organization, the meaning of Kaizen may be competitive advantage, to others it may mean customer satisfaction, to others it may mean lower costs, better quality, leaner processes, etc. The Meta-Coach ferrets out these meanings and coaches your executive, your middle manager, and your employee to align their meanings with the corporate meanings.

What it would look like

Whether you are an organization that is just starting to implement Kaizen or you are an organization that wants to get more out of your existing Kaizen program, you are constantly challenged with the efficiency demands of people, processes and tools. How do you fully utilize your executives, your middle managers, and your employees in the tools of Kaizen through the processes of Kaizen?

The first thing you do is ask yourself, why do people do anything? Why do they even wake up in the morning? Everyone wakes up, gets dressed, and starts their day. Why? Is there a theory of motivation that explains why people do what they do or are we left with just a willy-nilly let's get it done attitude? Chapter two of this book was about motivation and what motivates people. Motivation is movement to do something. There were different theories that were proposed in chapter two, but they can all be synergized into a needs based hierarchy. Within a needs based hierarchy you have the inclusion of the meanings of those needs and the needs are themselves goals, attained again through various meanings.

That hierarchy of needs is the Hierarchy of Needs as postulated by Abraham Maslow. According to that synergistic model, all people get up in the morning because they are somewhere on that hierarchy. They get up and move and get dressed etc. because they either are deficient in food, in safety, in social relationships, in self-esteem, or they need to grow and self-actualize. If we know that everyone, including your executive, your middle manager, and your employee gets up and comes to work because of a specific need, then we have the start of a plan for developing a Kaizen culture.

At an organizational level, the deficiency needs can be met. There is money for food, there is job security and pension for security (or just good pay), there is a culture for social relationships, and there is a place for advancement and improvement to meet the self-esteem needs. Those are activities or plans that are already in place; it just may be that it was never considered as such, or delivered as such.

The final level of motivation on the Hierarchy of Needs is the growth level; the self-actualization level. As has been noted, self-actualization is the making actual that which is potential. Self-actualization is the Kaizen of the individual. Self-actualization takes place as a process of growth and is facilitated by meaning and responsibility to that meaning. First develop the Kaizen in the individual, and the Kaizen in the office takes care of itself.

The facilitation of Kaizen in the individual (self-actualization) takes place through offering the appropriate resources (training, mentoring, coaching) and then a direct deliberate responsible transfer of those resources into rich meaningful challenging outlet.

This transfer of those resources into rich meaningful challenging outlet takes place through the Meta-Coaching process. It includes following and leading your executive, middle manager, and employee through the natural change process using the Axis of Change Model. Using the Axis of Change Model as a tool of change facilitation, the Meta-Coach uses the other seven models to bring about transformational change in your executive, middle manager, and employee.

The Meta-Coach, throughout the transformational process, uses the NLP Communication Model to track the representations of your executive, middle manager, and employee. The Meta-Coach facilitates these employees' movements within their frames and states and brings to mind those movies that engender that mind-body-emotion state that best facilitates their self-actualization and their best Kaizen state.

The Meta-Coach, throughout the transformational process, uses the Meta-States Model of Reflexivity to facilitate your executive, middle manager, and employee through there different states, their different meta states, and there meta, meta, states etc. The Meta-Coach and the employee design engineer their states to such a degree that they support the personal transformation of Kaizen, and thus the organizational transformation through Kaizen.

The Meta-Coach, throughout the transformational process, uses all the concepts of the benchmarking model. The Meta-Coach uses top notch listening skills, listen for that which is not spoken. The Meta-Coach uses supporting skills, crisp sharp questioning skills, penetrating meta-questioning skills that ferret out the higher frames of the employee. The Meta-Coach uses state inductions to facilitate the transformational changes that your executive, middle manager, and employee requires for personal and organizational Kaizen.

The Meta-Coach, throughout the transformational process, uses the Matrix Model for working systematically with your executive, middle manager, and employee to visit their personal matrix.

The Meta-Coach facilitates your executive, middle manager, and employee through their content matrix of self-identity and how that identity reflects their personal transformation toward Kaizen. The Meta-Coach facilitates the employees through their other content matrices of power, others, time, and the world. Power as it relates to their own personal resources for transformational change, others as it relates to how they experience others related to personal transformation, time and world as it applies to their personal, and then ultimately the corporate Kaizen initiative.

The Meta-Coach, throughout the transformational process, facilitates your executive, middle manager, and employee through the Self-Actualization Quadrants to facilitate rich and robust meanings for their skills and the resources for their skills that they have rich meanings for; with the intent of transforming the organization through their personal transformation and personal Kaizen (self-actualization)

The Meta-Coach, throughout the transformational process, will facilitate your executive, middle manager, and employee through the Matrix Business Plan where they will give thought and attention to their intention, their meanings, and their states, within the context of the contents of self, power, other, time, and world matrix.

This process, will bring about self-actualization in the individual, an ongoing process; a process of personal Kaizen. And, as the chapter on self-actualization has shown, the self-actualizing individual will have peak performance and that peak performance will further facilitate the Kaizen culture of the organization. The Meta-Coach will bring together the theories of motivation, the transfer of resources, and the deep rich meanings that are necessary for a Kaizen culture.

The uniqueness of the Meta-Coaching Kaizen Facilitation Process is based on an inward-out approach, and not an outward-in approach. A typical transfer of training of Kaizen tool is to train the employee, and then try to transfer what they learned into the organization, thus transforming the organization with the hope that the employee is transformed with it, thus creating a culture. This process has been an unsuccessful challenge of many organizations. The Meta-Coach Kaizen Facilitation Process works from the inside out; the inner game, then the outer game. Actualize your executive, your middle manager, and your employee in personal Kaizen (self-actualization) and then the organization is transformed by those who are transformed into a Kaizen culture, sustainable, and with a strong competitive advantage. Or, keep doing what you are doing. If you already have a competitive advantage and already have a culture of continuous improvement than congratulations, you are a one in a million company, but if you don't, then where is your matrix going to take you as you decide what decision to make now?

This process is more than just a coaching intervention process; it is a system of planned changes of leadership, motivation, transfer of training, culture, etc. It is my opinion that this system is best facilitated by a trained Meta-Coach. That being said, if you are interested in bringing this system together for a new Kaizen Culture here are a few options. 1.) You can send your leaders through Meta-Coach Training. 2.) You can have your leaders purchase and read Meta-Coach books. 3.) You can hire a Meta-Coach. 4.) You can contact me to consult and coach your leaders through this process. 5.) You can do a bit of all or some – the final question then becomes, what does all THIS mean to YOU?

Dr. Charles DesJardins, Ph.D.
www.drcharlesdesjardins@gmail.com

CPSIA information can be obtained at www.ICGtesting.com
Printed in the USA
BVOW04s1446091013

333325BV00017B/738/P